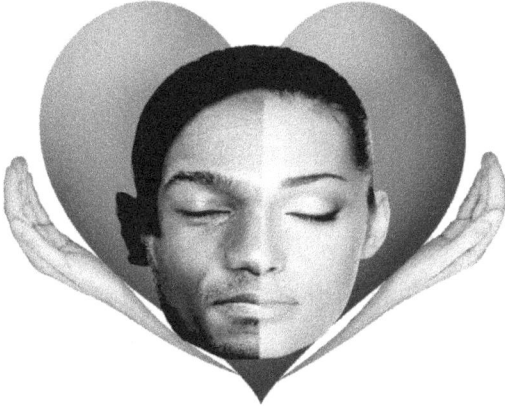

DREAMS OF LOVE

THATO
MOTCHELLO

First Printing: 2017

ISBN 978-0-620-73089-1

Contents

Dedication and acknowledgment

Most importantly, wholeheartedly, I love to appreciate you (the reader)—for your support and, giving yourself time to engage with this divine unparalleled message and connection. Without you, this book would not be inspired or exist—(Thank you).

To my mother, Tseleng Motchello, a woman of significance to me who has immensely believed in me and has helped to see this book through. With her support, understanding and backing, I was able to give time and finish this book.

Also, would like to give special grateful thanks to Sydwell Masilela for all the funding and financial support.

Finally to my good friend, Silver Modestus Ekene for showing up at the right time in my life and for bearing with me all this time (I appreciate you).

Preface

Dreams: We all have this deep great desire to live and achieve them. In sleep they are mysterious, and are full of oblique contradictory confusion to our reality. And we often wonder what they mean, and how we find ourselves in them. At times they can be a pleasing wonderful and a great experience of fantasy and desire. Yet and also, they can be awfully terrifying, horrific, and a complete nightmare of an experience.

Well, DREAMS OF LOVE is exactly for that. It solves this all-time universal mystery. It precisely explains how we find ourselves in a dream; and how to consciously gain and take control of our dreams when we are in their realm by manipulating its reality very aware. It gives the will power and solutions of how to live and achieve our most desired dreams in this world—by understanding that the connection of dreams and reality are one.

Most importantly, it shows and gives divine true reasoning that love is the creator of dreams. In fact love is the creator of everything in life (as you will soon find out when you read). Without love—this world and moment would not be alive and experienced.

SALUTATION

Hello, child! How are you doing today?
I am doing good, Parent.

What good have you done, child?
I am not sure I know how to answer that, Parent.

Well I tell you this: you have done well at and by living. You have yet awaken again to another moment of sun dawn as it resurrects new thoughts about you, and therefore you are doing living good that as such you thus say, "I am doing good." And that is the good you have done, child. You should be celebrating this moment.

Thank you, Parent, I did not realize it from that understanding.

Now that I have your utmost attention, I would like to tell you this. You do know that I love you, child.

Yes I do. But why are you telling me this here, dearest?

It is because I know that you are not clear of my love. Even though I have told you for so many moments of time continuously of how much I really do love you, still sometimes you forget that I do. And so now, I have decided to conclude and summarize my love for you in utter expression, so you may truly understand that I really do love you. Everything that we will touch up on, do, talk and converse about will be of and about love.

Okay, that is very interesting. I would love to hear all about it. But I thought you were going to help me understand my dreams better—how I find myself in a dream, and how to achieve them, along with my goals that I have for so long been aiming at. You said that you will help me become that which I desire to be without having to work hard for it, by giving me knowledge of dreams.

Yes, I will do that, child, and so now I say. I will help you understand dreams right now, right here, because I love you. Dreams are love making, and you love making dreams—(especially true). For you so much love your dream, you will do anything for it justly for the experience. You are doing what you love right now, and this is your dream unfolding to truth before you in at this exact present moment.

Now listen very carefully. Listen with your heart. Be with all your will and might for I am telling you how much I love you. I am sharing with you here right now, the great grandest story of all time. To the one that knows it, has heard and, remembers the story, is filled with understanding and love for its exact meaning. This is a story that the whole creation has been waiting on. It is the one that satisfies universal thirst. This is a true story that you have failed yourself, instead of giving yourself high grades, you rather settled to the lowest scores at the expense of your own right for wrong. And now, after this, you will rate yourself high, because you will realize the good that you have only done, to be where you are now.

Okay, please tell me. I must say that you got me so anxious and excited to hearing you tell this story. I am already prospecting and looking forward on to the read that follows, Parent.

Good, child. Now here it is.

THE STORY OF LOVE

Once upon a great moment in time, a billion and millions of thousands of years ago of current, there was, and still is, a child soul that wanted to have love, and its name was You. The child named You yearned for love so goodly with fueled ardour to have it. It desirously sought and relished nothing else other than love. The desire was as it is now, so great that it screamed from the air in the branches of its lungs pumping its divine breath of life. It screamed and shouted so loud that the earth in heaven shook and vibrated immensely.

"Hello! Can anyone hear me? Oh please, who is out there to give me love? Anybody! Somebody! Please give it to me. Is there not any being out there that is willing to give me? Hey, maybe you over there—or, how about you there, will you do it; will you give it to me? Yes you, will you give me love?" wailed the child soul, imploring with saddened anxious passion of desire.

Oh wait, that is not the end of it. In the mist of it all, along emerged two souls. They appeared from the great vast void that is all, which of is filled with draughty still warm waters of transparent nature that is without.
"Hey, we will give you love. Because you want it so goodly, we will give it to you. We love you so much that we are willing to give birth to you through love, so you may feel and know the experience as we create it." The two souls said sincerely with great devotion.

And so it is as it should be that, the two souls got together and set aside their difference. They got to know each other through love for love. They made love together, and indulged in it, thus it was made and created. And so it is as it should be that they gave love to their child through birth. The lovely created child was and is so beautiful, so immaculate and so magnificent in all aspects of perception. No fault, no wrong and far most importantly, no bad that is foul was intended or done, yet only love. And so it is as it should be that the soul child was and is perfect in all-ways. It was and is indeed perfectly love!

"Oh my, oh my sweet love, how good I feel! How so good it feels to have you. How nice it is to be love. Oh, oh my great love, I have you, you are mine now! I love you love. Oh, thank you so much great souls for giving me this. It is so good to me, I do not know what to do with it and to myself. Look everyone, everybody! Yes you, look, I have love." The child soul awesomely chanted.

And so it is as it should be that, the child soul found and had love that it wished and beseeched for. It was so happy, excited and full of overwhelming blissful joy. It went everywhere declaring it, and each moment was expressed as experienced frolic and in rapture. It was indeed happy because it was blessed with love, by two souls that offered the experience of it. The soul child settled for this great eternal fortune feeling of treasure.

Now then, as moments of love passed on, the child understood and accepted that it had love. It stopped its chanting, begging, and its declaration of it. The earth in heaven stood quite still and calm, there was peace, it was quiet and soundless. It did this because it knew that it had love. It had just plenty of only it and, that there was no need to ask for it or tell any other soul being about it in proclamation of majestic exhibited display. Since the soul child had a great grasp of this, it did not care as before for or about love in consideration, because that is the only thing it knows in having, and it will never ask for it again. And so as it is, that the soul child chose to forget in knowing about what it had, by ignoring it. You chose the experience of other things in the fore presence of love. It relished and swam in the transparent deep to float in pleasures of the great endless marvelous creation.

4

Now, after millions of billions of moments of time, the child thought of the love it had; it yearned for it again.

"Oh love, oh my sweet one and only love, where are you?" It queried heartedly, forgetting that it has it. Then again, from the mist of it all emerged the two loving souls.

"Hey, remember that you asked for love and we gave you the experience of it in creation to be? Now we say unto you, remember that you have it. Go now, quick! Go find it where you left it, in your memory." The two loving souls solemnly said, with dazzling countenance.

And so as it is that it should be, the soul child left to find love. It went to places about on earth within the universe, looking and searching relentlessly everywhere for love until it had found it in the place of memory.

"Oh I remember, here it is! Oh my good sweet, I found it, I finally found it. It was always with me, I had just forgotten about it. Oh, how I feel complete again, I feel so great again. I am the great eternal love!" You said in proclamation. There was palpitation of jubilation in its body. Love was felt the same as it was always before.

"Good is what you have done. You have done good for finding it as you always have. And now we say unto you again, do not ever forget it that you have as you are love." The two loving souls said.

"Oh thank you so much, thank you so greatly! I will not forget love." The Soul child called You echoed gratitude. And so as it is that it should be, there was love again.

But wait, it does not end there. Now again as before, with the love that You had, it so wished and desired to give it to another beautiful soul. It wanted to give some other soul what it had and is experiencing from love. You wanted by wish, to have a relation with any soul that is willing by choice, to know and understand the same experience of this eternal great feeling fuming essence of sweet rose aroma captured by replenishing morning dew dropping from a petal, quenching the universe in reinvigoration.

"Hello!" it shouted, "Hello! Is anyone out there? Is there any soul being that would like to feel love? Does any being want this beautiful and majestic thing called love? I would like to give my love to someone so we may relate to it in feeling." The soul child echoed with subtle-striking rainbow colors of queries.

You so goodly and willingly wanted to give this good feeling to someone, some being of soul that needs love to experience it just as it did before, and now! Oh well, just as before, again, in the mist of it all emerged another young beautiful adorable soul.

"Hey, I will take it. I need love so badly that it is the only one thing that I care about. I do not need anything else but love. Please, please show it to me! Give it to me, I will have it." This other beautiful soul eagerly said.

And so as it is that it should be that love was given to it by a soul child called You.

Hum ⋯ How long is this going to take Parent?

Be patient, child. I told you that I am telling the greatest story of all universal time. Now listen with your witty heart.

Okay.

As time passed in moments, the soul child called You, longed for his love. It screamed and shouted so loud again unto the earth that is in heaven. It pleaded, fell on its knees and wailed in intense demonstrations of agony; wetting, scratching and scraping the great earthly ground for its love back.

"Oh love, Oh my one and only sweet love that I had, please come back to me. Please!" the soul child pleaded.

And again the two souls emerged.

"Hey, we gave you love. Remember that you cannot and will never lose it for you will always have it. Now what did you do with it?" asked the two parent souls.

"I gave it to another beautiful soul that needed it just as good as I did, so we may relate to it in understanding, together. I thought of it to be a good thing to give love to someone who does not have." The soul child called You said.

"Now, we say unto to you. Go! Go now, child, and take it from where you gave it." The two parents said.

The soul child went about on earth in heaven, seeking and searching to take back its love from whom it had given to. It went about, until it found and met with the other adorable beautiful soul.

"Hey!" It called, "I am here to take and claim back my love."

"No! Please do not take it. You cannot take this away from me, you gave it to me. Please, please, I beg of you do not take it. It is so good to be loved, it is so good to have love. What will I do without it?" The other beautiful soul child pleaded with glint eyes of tears filled with drops of bitter-lemon taste from heart with You.

The other beautiful soul was now rueful to have accepted and taken good benevolent gesture of love from You, because it now sees and knows by feeling of how it is like to lose and be without love. The two souls were both in a melancholic state and misery because they both did not want to lose and be without love. Now then, it is within in this grand moment of love that is now, that the child soul named You, came to a great realization, and understood love. You remembered that it was, and will always be love. It remembered that it was made from and out of love, and therefore cannot be without, for it is.

"From now on, I will not forget my love. I will not give love. From now on until to the moment of my existence, I will only share my love to all beautiful souls that choose to have it with me. I will be nothing else other than love that is shared. I will forever be love. I am love!" The soul child proclaimed from the concentric universe.

And, the end!
Wow, now that was and is a great story, Parent.

Mm, Yes I know, and I will tell you why I shared that story with you, child. I will give all rational reasoning to put you on full ultimate realized clarity of how much I have always been there, and now here, with love, to and for you for love.

Okay, I am listening, tell me. But before you do that, I have so many questions to ask you, I really do have a lot to ask.

And I will tell you this, I have a lot to answer, child. I will give you all the answers that you think to need.

Thank you. Now can you tell me?

I am ⋯ and I tell you this: love can and will always be shared. Love cannot not be shared. The reason why I told you that story is because sharing is caring. You only share what you have with someone or some being because you care for them or it so much, that you will share what you have with them or it. And you only do this, because you love them or it. Since they or it thinks it does not have what you have, you give it willingly out of love as you care and, promised yourself to, for the experience.

Okay cool. Let me see if I understand what you are saying, Parent. So according to you, is that I do have love?

Yes, you do, child.
I do have love because it was given to me by two souls that had it?

No and yes. No it was not given, it was shared with you for the same experience in relation of understanding the feeling together. If it was all given to you, then those who gave it to you would and cannot love you now, because they will not have love, as they would have given it all away to you. And therefore they would not have a feeling of it towards you as they would not possess it, since that you would be the only one who is feeling it. And yes they have given it to you, only a sum of its totality as to so you may have some of it. And also know this; love cannot be finished because there is only one of its kind, which means there is no any other but it, and only that one love is for all to have in plenty. So everybody tuck in and eat from this one love for all.

Okay, I hear you, Parent. Thanks!

And this is when I say it is a pleasure. It is a pleasure because it really does please me when you understand. And now you are welcomed, all of you are welcomed, child.

Thank you once more, Parent.

It is a great universal pleasure, child.

I tell you this: there is also a soul that shouts from a distance afar. It cries and calls out for love. It utters and says, "Who loves me so much that they will stand in front of a bullet for me. Is there any one soul that loves me, that it will sacrifice to take its life being for me, and is willing to take a bullet for it?" And in the mist of it all there is as always, a soul that appears and is willing to give and show the experience of love, only love and nothing else, to the other in kindness. A soul comes to being in a form that you know as human being. It sacrifices all that is as it is love. It takes the lowest of highest form of being, just to give the experience of yearned love by the other soul to experience it.

This is why you will and would find a man or a woman full of soul, standing bravely in front of someone they love ardently before a bullet, as to protect them. They do this because of the promise they give to the other soul to experience love the way it wishes it. Now I tell you this, this is the reason why you would and will cry when it happens that you feel losing something that you love. It is so because you are experiencing the love, of which is by feeling of any sort that you wished for when you were calling it out. Because you asked love to show and prove itself of how it really loves you, according to your desires of love experience, it thus fills your whole yearning soul being completely with itself magnificently as so you may experience it. Now, you should rejoice in love and not in grave sad pain of tears, because your wish has been lovingly fulfilled.

Wow, so that is it? You mean I should be happy when someone dies for me, Parent?

Well I tell you this, you should be thankful that you have received such much love as you have been asking for it. Oh my child, your desire to experience love entirely in all its forms, for it to reveal, prove and show its true loving kind nature of any circumstantial-situational requested experience, has produced suicides, fights, accidents, abuse, rape, war, stabbing, cunning trickery and all leading to death.

Hum ⋯ wow this is some news of substantial information. I am grateful, and therefore I feel to say, thank you, Parent.

Then that is our next talk after this, child.

What?
Being thankful, child!

Now listen for this is reason. Because of this deeply soaked desire to feel and experience love. You are drawn and caught up in the love vortex itself by yourself, to experience all of it wholly in anyway. Because of the same (relative) reason, you have chosen to need and require what you have already, which is love, to be attentive to you. And just only by thinking, because when you think it is not being attentive, you say you do not feel it. You even claim in your own words that it does not exist, while in your full knowledge and understanding, realize that it does exist as you wish it to be, in request of manifestation.

Wait ⋯ hold on, you mean to say that I seek attention from love for love, Parent?

Yes you do, child. You seek attention from the one that really loves you. You ask, and cry out to the one that loves you to listen to you, if not, you say that one does not really do. You say to the ones that really love you, that they do not love you because they were never there as a certain figure during the course of your upbringing, and that they have never done anything for you. Forgetting that, that is the very one that had thee out of love—for love to be

11

experienced by feeling it as it is requested from the thought of none existence and need of desire.

I tell you this, you have asked and expected gifts and things from the one that really loves you, and when you do not get, you say that one does not really completely and devotedly whole heartedly love you. And whenever that one devotedly and completely loves you, by following every say of word, instruction, command and desire of any pleasure, to give and have you what want without questioning or refusing it, you say to the one that loves you that, their love is hypocritical. That they are stupid and not enough of who they are, for doing and giving what you want all the time. You be, feel, do and say these, because you know and realize that when you have all that you want all the time, you cannot experience it because you know you already have it, thus as such you choose what you want from all that you have already in this world very cautiously, right now as you live.

Mm ⋯ wow, I ⋯ hum ⋯ what should I say? I am overwhelmingly taken by both breath and word. I am out of it, yet I feel to say that I do get it. I really do understand your love.

Good, child. You are doing very good now.
Thank you, Parent.

Now I tell you this, the same feelings you have of love and about it, came directly from love. Therefore listen when I say this, so you may understand and be clear – and it is not the last time nor is it the first time. Now, this is what this one says; I say unto you:

I Love You

THANK YOU – IT IS A PLEASURE

This is what love says

Now listen with all your heart. Listen with both ears and let all your eyes be focused and be present in soul, because what follows is divine truth of universe' s soul.

Okay, thank you, I am listening Parent.

Have you ever wondered why you say what you have just said, child?
Hum, no! What did I say?

You just said "thank you", remember? And do you know why you say that child?

Hum ⋯ ah ⋯ I don' t know.
You do not know why you say "thank you," child?

Well it is because you are presenting me with information, you are giving me knowledge and understanding of stuff, and that is what I have always wanted and that is why I say, 'thank you' . I say that because now I understand.

Good, child, great! You are doing good. Now listen to this, yes you do say thank you when you receive to have. You say thank you because you now have it. You have that which it is that you have been looking for, wanting, searching and desiring to have all this time. This is the reason why you would say thank you to someone who gives you what you want. (*Thank you*) is a very big meaningful word, and therefore you should be carefully observant of what and to whom you say thank you to.

Okay, I get that, Parent.

Good. Now listen to this as well: *Pleasure*, and *thanks*, or *thank you*, go hand in hand together. When someone says that, "it is a pleasure" that simply means that he or she or they, enjoy what they are doing, and they are only doing it for pleasure and out of pleasure. It pleases and makes them happy. Happiness comes from the things you do out of love for you to receive its pleasure. This simply means that when doing what you love to and or for yourself or to someone, you receive its pleasures of that love, and this is why you would say that "it is only a pleasure." Indeed it is a pleasure because you love it. It is a pleasure because it makes you happy, and also it is a pleasure because that other important person you gave it to is also happy and, that makes you even merrier to give it to him or her, whatever it is they are thankful for. So yes, you should also be carefully observant to and for what you say it pleases you. Just like with (*thanks or, thank you*), *pleasure* is also a big word and it should not be taken for nothing. Therefore only say it is a pleasure when you are happy and you truly love what you are receiving and or giving in pleasure. And also, only say thank you when you are receiving and or giving what you truly love.

I tell you this: there is no true pleasure in doing what you do not love. When you do what you do not want or love, and you end up saying that "it is a pleasure," it is only because that which you do not want, like or love, gives you what pleases you.

Okay ⋯ I am not sure I understand, please elaborate on that Parent.

Good, follow me and keep up, child. Now listen again, when you do something that you do not truly wish for, want, like or love, and in the process of doing it, you receive tons and loads of a lot of money for it, this is the only time you will say it is a pleasure. You say it is a pleasure because you are pleased with or of how much you get for doing what you do not wish, like and love. You put aside the true fact that you do not like doing it, and put first before you what pleases you, and in this case, (which in most cases is always the case), and that is money.

You will and would do anything for money. You have and do put your life in danger, risk and prioritize money first. You have told yourself and you still do; you say that money rules, and yet you have not taken enough time to see who is in control and ruling money. And I tell you this, you will and can have a dime now, and you will show to yourself and the world at large before you now, of how you rule that one dime by commanding it to have you what you wish and want on its expense. You are the one who is in charge of that dime, and you get to decide what to do with it. And guess what? That dime has no say in the matter because all authority is unto to you to rule over it, as created.

Now listen, because you said it was and is a pleasure, you will then do what you do not want as many times as you choose, only to get the pleasure of getting more money from it. And this is why you say it is a pleasure in doing what you do not like or love. And indeed since you are pleased with what you get from doing what you do not like or love, you will also say "thank you" for the pleasure of money.

Mm ⋯ I do hear you Parent.
Good, well done. You see, you are doing good after all.

Thanks.
It is a pleasure, child.

Now look and listen child. The only way to be wholly, fully, quite utterly and truly happily pleased, is when you receive pleasure from doing what you love, and get paid tons, loads and lots of money for it. Oh, and yes, as a Parent, I do know that you will and would argue that, but there are people who do what they love and do not get paid enough money for it, and some do not even get paid at all. And I will tell you this—it is because they are not doing what they love for themselves in heart, instead they are doing what they love for someone, to that person's pleasure.

So are you saying that I should not do what I love for someone else, Parent?

Well I tell you this: I am only saying that do it when it is a pleasure. When what you are doing is what you love, and you are not pleased with what you get and to whom you are doing it to or for (in that moment), then you should choose not do it, and to them because you do not get your pleasure out of it, even if you love it. And when you do say it is a pleasure, then you are fooling yourself because only you know from pits deep bottom of your heart that you are not pleased with what you get.

I tell you this: when you do it for yourself, then there is no expectation. The only thing you should expect when you do something for yourself, is the very same amount of input being outputted. This is to say that, the amount, energy and efforts that you put in to something, equals its output.

Oh my God, are we going into the deep stuff already?

You asked for this, now brace yourself as there is much truth about to come from this. Get ready child, you are partaking in the greatest journey of self and it is about to get worse better than now.

And I thought we were going to talk deeper about dreams, Parent.

Yes we are, and this is the path to your dreams. Remember that love is dreams and dreams are love. You are making love to your dreams, now.

Now look and listen. Listen with your heart and be present in soul. And now I tell you this: The words *thank you*, *thanks* or *pleasure*, are glorious words. They are glorious because there is a level of joy or happiness at some degree that is experienced and, it is celebrated when these words are used. In most if not many cases, this joy and or happiness is suppressed by you because of regarding it as less important for money, and thus it is not felt to that degree of expected joy and or happiness when it should be. Joy and or happiness is a result of pleasure or thanks, thus therefore only when you truly remember and understand by observing, why you would say or use the words (*thanks*, *thank you* or, *it's a pleasure*)—in your everyday life, you would be happy every moment, every second and every now because you will realize that you are receiving your happiness.

I hear what you are saying Parent, but I am not sure if I understand.
Good, I will explain it to your simplest understanding then, child.

Every day and every moment when you say, "thank you" or "it is a pleasure", you should take a moment and be still child. Take pause, be calm and look back as to why you had or have just said *thank you* or *it's a pleasure*. Do this and you will see how beautiful it is. How truly divine and majestic it is in its glory of the gift you just gave to or receive.

You see, the words (*It is a pleasure*) are an acknowledgement and awareness of received and or given experience to meet its highest desired choice in fulfillment. And the words (*Thank you*) are an acknowledgement that you have received pleasure and therefore you are happy. And since you are happy, you thus give back from where you have received with and in thanks. And also in contrast in your daily vocabulary, you use the words (*no thank you*), well for obvious reasons as to reject what is or has been given to one, as

17

it is not part of perceived desired dream in lineage to itself in the moment. And now I say unto you, take time, be still, calm and stable. Take a moment and observe who, why and what is given, and see if you truly are gratefully pleased in thanks.

I say this child: Observe and be aware of how much money is paid to you. Is that how much you are worth of value, are you really happy with that? Will you say thank you or no thank you? Is it the love of it that makes it a path to your dreams? Observe and be aware of why and who is passing to hand you that bottle or glass of liquor to drink in the moment. And is it part of your dream, will you say thank you, or no thank you? Is that your friend or does that person really love you? Observe and be aware of why and who is passing to you that joint of cannabis-weed, crack, cocaine or tobacco to smoke. And is it part of your dream, will you say thank you, or no thank you? Is that your friend or does that person really love you? Observe and be aware of why and who you are plotting or scheming with to steal, break in, rape, rob and or to kill. See if it is part of your dream, and will you say thank you, or no thank you? Is that your friend, or does that person really love you?

Every time, child, and every moment when you receive anything in your hands, you should have a great good look at it as to what it is and its purpose of serving to where you really think lies your true ultimate dreams about yourself before you say thank you. Because when you say thank you to what is not part of your dreams, you affirm and accept that you have received what makes you happy. And just like we said before, it means that there is a level of joy or happiness at some degree that is experienced. There is a part of you that is celebrating from having received what is in hand (no matter how little that joy may be), and since you are so thankful for it that you say *thank you*, then the more of its overflow abundance will fill your hands of your life, even if it comes from where or what your dreams are not ultimately realized.

Mm ⋯ interesting! I am listening. I am present with and in soul Parent.

Good, very good child.

Now to truly see that I do understand you; are you saying that everything that I have, and gained through my life existence is because I said thank you to it in acceptance, Parent?

Yes! Because when you would have said "no thank you" as to reject the gift that is not part of your dreams rather than accept it, you would not have it now, in possession, child! And also when you would have said "it is not a pleasure" as to reject the unpleasant experience of what is not part of your dream, you would not have that experience now, child.

Wow, that is good to know and very chill alerting, Parent. Phew ⋯ oh ⋯ okay, so are you saying that the life that I am living now, the life that I so much think is so good and joyous, and yet depressing, shameful, regretful and such a struggle to maintain and, have the true experience of where I see myself, as to where my dream is, is only because I said 'thank you' to it? Only because I accepted a gift I do not like because of its pleasures that are not part of my dreams?

Yes, child.
So what do I have to do, what can I do to change all of it to my true dream?

Well I think we both know that you do know and have the answer to that, child. This is after all a no brainer.

Okay I see ⋯ and all I have to do or say is (no thank you), to the experience of the given gift of where I do not see myself, or as to where my true dream is.

Yes you do get it, you do understand. Yes that is exactly what you should choose to do or say. Just say "no thank you" to the unpleasant experience

19

of what is not, and say "thank you" to the pleasant experience that serves your true pleasurable, desirable and loving dream that is.

Oh my goodness, is it that simple? All that I have to say is "no thank you," and move on?

Yes, child, that is all you have to say.

Wow, this (*thanks, thank you, no thank you, pleasure* or, *it's a pleasure)* stuff, really is complicated right? I mean would it not seem mean and rude to other people, isn't it offensive or a disposition of ungratefulness, or a bad thing to refuse and reject what is given out of love?

Well I tell you this: it is not when it is dependent to your true ultimate desired dream. When the one whom you call Jesus, would have accepted what was offered to him kindly out of love (nothing else but love), to have all the riches of the world, by the one whom you call the devil, in request to have the same dream as Jesus, he would not be where he is now. But because he knew and realized his dream, from a young age, he rejected what was not, and thus lived and died his dream on the cross as it is and planned, and this does not make him mean or rude at all to have rejected. And when people or someone does get offended by you rejecting the presented gift, no matter how good, big or beautiful it is, it is because they mean to offend your dream. They mean to put you far off-end of your dream as to not achieve it.

And now I say unto you again child, you have all the power, the might and right to say, "no thank you, I will not have it," and "it is not a pleasure," no matter how good or beautiful it is, when it is not part of your true ultimate realized dream as to where you want and choose to be in life. And I do promise you that it does not make you mean, offending or rude at all to reject something. For you to accept any gift of sort as so not to hurt the giver, means that you hurt the most precious thing held closely to your heart, which is your dream.

Every single thing, no matter what it is and how simple or precious it is, it is a gift given in and out of love, child.

I see, and I do hear you. I do understand. And now I ask for your help. Help me understand more of how to accept or reject a gift without hurting, wounding or derailing my dream off in the moment, and the person that gives the gift. Help me, Parent.

I am here child. Now I say unto you: For you to be able to accept or reject a gift without derailing your dream and hurting the person that gives the gift. You have to be decisively clear and singularly truly honest of or with who you are in your dream. By this, I simply mean that you have to be honest of what you want and not lie to yourself. Since you will be and are fully clearly honest with yourself, you will tell your mother, father, sister and or brother and friends. You will tell everybody and anybody of who you honestly truly are to yourself and, the things that you do not want in your life book of honest truth about yourself to your dream.

Wow that is good to know … please carry on I am still listening.
Good child.

Now since you are truthfully honestly clear about yourself to yourself and everybody you know and have met in your life, in this moment. You will first not give yourself a gift that you dislike, hate or do not love. This simply means that you will not go buy or get for yourself what you do not truly honestly want to be given to you as a gift by someone. And also the same applies towards the people whom you became truthfully honestly clear about yourself to. They will, secondly after you first, not buy or give a gift that you were so honestly clear about from the start, that you do not want it in your ultimate realized dream of where you choose to be in life in relation to it.

Now I tell you this: To all the people you were and are honestly clear about your true self to. Should they in their full knowing of who you are, offer you what you do not like or want, and you reject the gift or offer that is given truly out of love by saying "no thank you," to it as to refuse the gift that is on offer, and they end up feeling offended by your refusal, and insisting in persistence for you to have it. It is only because they intend to off-end and harm your dream of who you are out of and in their love. In their love for it, and thus it is so that they feel what they give, which is offense.

Wait ⋯ wait, wait; you just wait and hold it here. When you stress and emphasize that "in their love – " are you saying that they are offending me out of love? Are you saying even if they honestly fully know who I am, and what they offer is highly or lowly against my dream, is only out of love, Parent?

Yes! It is so. Remember the story of love I told you of? Remember that love is everything and, thus this is the dream you love. I tell you this, remember the story of the one child soul that goes by the name You. I told you that everything we will talk about and touch on is love. I said that I will make you understand and be clear of my love, child.

Yah, yah ⋯ yes I do remember, please do continue.

Good. Now I say this again, yes all gifts are given out of love. When a person that truly honestly knows you, gives you something that he or she knows you do not like or love to have in the experience of your dream in persistence, and feels offended by the rejection in – no thank you, then that means that person only loves one thing for you.

Okay ⋯ and what is that?

That person only has one love for you. He or she would really ⋯ really love to see you fall off-end to your dream. He or she would really be happy and pleased to see you fall on your lowest as to your knees. He or she tells herself or himself that she or he really loves to see you fall, in gossip with others.

And this is the same as it was with whom you call Jesus. Because the one whom you call the devil, out of his love to see Jesus fall and on his knees worshiping him, he offered all the worldly riches as a gift and in test.

I tell you this, it is in such gifts and moments of time that you should really be still, calm, clear and observe and, be aware why and whom is giving you a gift. Will you say, "Thanks" and or, "no thank you" or "I am pleased" ? Is that your friend or does that person really love you? It is within such times you should raise your head and look into the persons eyes and see who your true honest friends are, towards the dream you see yourself in.

Wow, now that was intense Parent!

Tell you what child? How about or you grab a glass of water, wine, milk, beer or juice just to relax a bit. I mean I do not want to make your brain pop like heated corn.

Yah, now that would be great ⋯ I need some.

Wait! Before you say it, let me say that it is a pleasure, child.
And let me say, "thank you" Parent.

Good.

And now I ask you, child. Where do you choose to be, and what will you accept and give thanks to? Will you accept yourself as a person that sleeps around having sex, and give thanks when paid or given something, or you want nothing at all from the ones you sleep with? Do you accept yourself as a soldier that goes to war and kills people and gives thanks when paid and honored? Do you accept yourself as a great ruler of a leader that never listens to the greater mass of the people in aching agony for radical change to better their lives, and still give thanks when paid? What is your true dream, and to what measures of any circumstance will it take for you to get it? Will you accept yourself as a drunkard and give thanks every time you buy or are given alcohol? Who are you in this great dream of you and about yourself in the universe, child?

Wow ⋯ now I really do not know because I am not sure. I have never concluded the life I am, in my dream. I have just been trying whatever it is I can do, and then move to the next thing. I try this and then change my mind later, no matter how long it is I have been on that thing.

I know child. I just wanted you to have a moment of self. Yet I will help you to answer these questions as I unfold universal truths to you. I will tell you what and who you are in your ultimate true honest realized dream of self.

Thank you, Parent.
It is a pleasure, child.

VALUE OF WORTH

This is what love says

The greatest there ever is – the one that I pride myself with love. Oh my child, the one that affords to clothe self with expensive crystal sparkling, and twinkling diamond of jewels that shine on the dark body of the universe. My beautiful one that no cost amounts to, because of only nothing is worth great value to the magnificent glorious treasure that you are already. My rich and wealthy child, the one that has never been less of more than what one is now. You are rich!

Wow ⋯ now that, right there, just made feel a whole lot more rich than I am right now. I just felt like going out there, and spend money on the things I would really like, right now. A sad short story is that, I know I do not have enough to get and have some of those things I desire and really want in life, Parent.

I am in total knowledge of that. I know that you think, say, see, feel, know and even believe that you do not have enough, child. Now listen, be present, organize and put all feelings of desire together in order as so they may be met. I am about to tell again of how you settle for that which you have now, by self-worthiness and value of evaluation.

Now I tell you this: You are in this current situation of thinking and then knowing that you do not have enough, because you have settled for it. Most of many frequent times, you settle because of what you have received still sustains and sees you to another day, in your current living situation. Well and of course, we do know by now that, whatever you have now, you thus accepted it and gave thanks for it, because of some pleasures you got out from it.

You rise to a day excited, from saddened realities of past days, full of hope to get more of the little that was enough to get you through a day from the previous, and then think to yourself that you do not have enough. And yet still go back to that place, thing and or person that gave you the very little that was enough to get you through the previous day. This is to simply say that, you look forward to a day hoping for more, yet going back and doing the same that did not give you more of what you keep on hoping for. Now I tell you this; you are not even aware that you do have enough, and always have had. That which has been sustaining you through some durable time of your life till to this point, is the one thing that has been enough for you.

Whoa ⋯ wow, slow down, Parent. You are hitting me hard, and banging on the right places on me here. All these seem to be right, and I can't take them all in at once. So please just take it easy there.

Banging? Oh I see, ah ⋯ some humor in you, nice touch, I like it. I know and believe that we both needed that here, dearest child.

Yah, we kind of did, Parent.

Good, you still are doing good I see. Now listen, be bearing with me, because I am about to hit you harder than I have, with truth that shocks you to perplexity.

In order for not enough to exist, a span of that which has been received and accepted, (which in this case), is what has been enough for you, in your settlement for it, is reduced to a certain rationalized specific required time.

Okay ⋯ wait, so what do you mean by that, Parent?

This is what I mean, by saying it. Whatever it is that you receive and accept, even though it is enough, you willingly think and choose to see as you believe, and decide that it is not enough, because of how long it takes to have in acquiring it, in the time period you agreed on and accepted. For a particular acquired thing to be enough, in the instance of thirty-one-days, that very same thing can be acquired in every sixteen days instead. Should you also again, decide that it is not enough by thinking so, within that sixteen days, it can be acquired in every eight days. This process of span reduction or expansion can and will continue, until you ultimately choose and decide that it is now enough, to receive something at every particular moment of certain preferred shrunk time, rate and interval.

Now, in your life time, the average mode of you receiving money that you agreed on has been thirty-one-days. It has been so, because you settled for it. You wait every month, patiently and impatiently, for an average of thirty-one-days to receive a certain lump bundle amount of money. I tell you this, that very same amount of money can and will be had on different time period rate of choice.

Wow ⋯ okay. I do hear you Parent.
Good, Child.

I listened and heard to what you said. I have been very attentive, my good Parent. So ⋯ from what you have said, you mean that whatever amount of money that I have received as a payment is already enough. It is already enough because I agreed, accepted and settled for it. I agreed on this, mostly averagely in the span of each thirty one days, annually, in my life. I also agreed on this because it was enough to get me by through each one day of thirty-one, hence I thus go back to work for another month, to receive the very same amount, that gets me through to another. In other words I have been doing good, and that's why I am still alive to this day?

27

Correct! Spot on. You have got it, child. Good, very good.

Okay, wow. Now also, you say that it becomes "not enough", because I willingly, as free minded and spirited as I am, think, choose, decide and even believe that it is not enough, because of how long it takes to have it, for the things I want to do and have in the current moment now when I want. For that very same amount that is already enough, in payment, and that I think it is not enough; for it to be enough again, the time period it is received in, would have to be reduced, to bring it nearer or closer to a certain specific required time by shrinking (or maybe stretch to make it longer). Which means I would have to change and re-settle differently again—instead of thirty one, but rather choose lesser or more if suitable. Also this process can and will continue until I fully, ultimately decide that ⋯ okay ⋯ maybe it's just about time, for that very same amount to be enough now, and call it quits!

Yes! Exactly that, you do get it. That is exactly what you are doing now, in your life, child.

Okay, now let us be directly clear about it, Parent. So you are saying that I choose to go work, for at most equally to least, for thirty-one-days.

Yes, child.

Okay, and in these thirty-one-days, I settle for a certain particular agreement of payment, from where I am receiving it.

Yes, my good child.

Okay, I am still good. So whatever the amount is, it is enough to get me through a day to the next. But for it not to be enough, as I think, it is because I wait a long thirty-one-days, to get the very same amount. Yet and also for it to be enough again as I would like, I have to re-think of a different sooner and closer week, of that thirty-one, on a certain day. Well and if that is the case, I can have that same amount that I am being paid monthly—every week, day, hourly, or even every second and or millisecond or nanosecond. I can do this —enough and, not enough thingy until I am fed up with it, and that is to say, until I am enough. So in a sense, I am forever rich, and only on my command and will, do I stop being, and say that it is enough dependently on span. Because if and when I get what I am normally paid in thirty-one-days every second, then I will be a billionaire.

Bravo! Well done, you do have it. And is that a smile that I see on your face? Oh wow, look at you feeling all good and stuff.

Well, what can I say, Parent. I receive and take from the best.

Oh very well then, shall we continue good child.
Well of course, after you, Parent.

Yes my good child. You have evaluated, and concluded what you are worth of and value to. To truly see and be aware of what value of worth you have placed for yourself, by agreeing to settle on what you are being paid, on contract of clear written terms. Take a good look at your pay after thirty one days when you receive it. Ask yourself if you truly are happy, see if your mind thinks that it is enough or not. And if it is, or not, do you truly know and believe that you are worth of value to that?

I see what you are getting at, and I hear you, Parent. But what am I supposed to do? Should, I give my own amount that I think I deserve and, is worth of great value for me, to my employer, just because of that I think and feel that he, or she or they are paying me a little?

Remember, child, that the money is enough ⋯ but not ideal to wait for it for thirty-one-days, or even longer than that, for your convenience—

29

Yah ⋯ yah ⋯ yah, enough with that already, I got that part, Parent.

Well I tell you this, yes you should choose to bring your own self-satisfying value of worth to the table, child.

Well we both know, Parent, unless you pretend not to – that you do not know. I do know that the chances to that happening, are as slim and thin as a thread, and one close to zero than a hundred percent. That hardly ever happens.

Well I tell you this: If the employer does not agree to your terms, then we both know, unless you pretend not to—that you do not know. I know and see of what he or she thinks of you, by the amount she or he values you worth of. And if you agree to that, just as you have done before, then we clearly see what you think of yourself, and what value of worth you are.

Well, I guess you got me on that one, Parent.

It is not to get back at you, or anything of such, child, yet only just to make you understand and aware of who you are in your dream.

Thank you once more, Parent.
It is a pleasure, my loved one.

Now tell me, should I therefore then leave it, or quit my job, if what is on offer is not worth of my value? What will I do next to survive and live, to maintain myself sustainably through to the next day? How do I get and live my value of worth, quickly thereafter quitting.

I tell you this child: The only barrier here is clouds of mist before your eyes that can be passed and walked through. It is the uncertainty of factual truthful possibility of what really exists of you beyond the mist. By this, I mean that you are not sure of yourself. You have not taken time to realize, this is to say, put into reality of who you are in this moment, and how long you will to be that which you choose.

You have highly considered and acted out what others suggested and recommended subjectively of what would be and is a great deal worth of value for you and appropriate, child. Value of worth is the true beloved ultimate awareness of self-creation of a certain unique particular action of a thing. Now, by this I mean that your skill of talent, that you are ultimately aware of and realize by particularly and uniquely self-creating out of true love for it and in doing, is value of worth.

Right now in your moment of time, child, you have put high value of worth on money, instead of your skill of talent. You love a lot of money thus you put extra zeros to have it changed to seven figures or more. Most widely large part of your life, you love to gain a lot of money over what you do for it, and how or what you create for it. This simply means that, as compared to money, you do not love your skill of talent that you are self-creating out of awareness in the moment, hence you are not sure, aware and clear and even have not put to reality of what your true ultimate beloved skill of talent is, in your dream, even though it is there and known to you by you.

Now, to respond and give an answer to your question whether if you should quit your work of job or not, and what to do if so or not; you have to be sure, clear, fully, ultimately and consciously realize who you truly are in this moment of self-creativeness, and put yourself to a high of low standard of value of worth.

Once and when you are sure of yourself in this moment now, you can and will to choose to stay in your work, and show to prove to yourself your certainty of assurance about yourself, of your skill of talent to your employers now in this moment. And should he or she, or they fail to recognize or not approve you assurance, then you should choose to quit your work to and for the value of worth that you know, see, believe in and consider yourself to be worth of, by thinking. You should choose to quit because you will be sure of who you are, in relation to your dream. You now know who you are and that you can do it, in this moment. You will walk through the hazy clouds of mist, because even though you do not see beyond it, yet you know what is beyond it, and that is you. Simply because you have, now, in this second, realized who you truly ultimately are!

Wow ⋯ once again. I am out of words. You just take them all out my breath, Parent. Thank you for all of this. I appreciate it. Wow, so this is how it really is hey? I mean I never think of it in this way.

It is always a pleasure my good child. I love to give you all that you think, and believe you need, child. This is my dream and I am living it. I have given you everything you have asked for, and I will do so until on, justly because I love you child, and I will to, unconditionally.

Thank you again. Oh thank you so much, Parent.

I tell you this, my good child. In ultimate truth no one can really afford you. You are just too great, and therefor that makes you too expensive. I tell you this; you are made from and of the colossal universe. It took a long great deal of now time, to create you now instantly in this moment. Your true value of worth is the universe itself, and that is how much it has caused to create you. You are just simply unaffordable, child.

Wow ⋯ so I am rich. I am rich beyond ⋯ I don't even know what to say. Just say rich of the universe, child.

Okay, thank you. I now understand ⋯ I do get it. Thanks to you, Parent. Good, very good.

Now I have another question, my good Parent.

I know, my good child. And I already have the answer for it.

Now tell me here, dearest Parent. Why do I sometimes find myself, in a desperate begging situation, or of asking someone for money to survive or to attain, get or gain something I think I need in the moment of now?

Now listen child, the answer to this question, and the next one you are about to ask, is very simple. You see it all boils and goes back to knowing yourself and how you value your worth. First of all, you find yourself in a begging situation because you do not see and are not clear of your skill of talent and to what value of worth it is, in your dream—you are way far out of your dream. If you were aware of it, you would live and give it, and thus receive something or some amount in compensation from your dream. Also whatever it is that you beg for, it is what you have placed value of worth on to yourself. When you beg for some few coins of little change, that is what you are worth of, if not, then just like I said, show and prove to yourself of what value of worth you are, (since that you already do have what it takes, like everyone).

Now, my child, you find yourself begging because you are not giving. If you were giving your true beloved skill of talent in assurance, from what you are in your dream, to someone, you would receive something without asking for it, or begging for it, on behalf of what you have done in return deservingly from the love that the other person feels, to reciprocate.

Wow ⋯ okay, I do get that one as well.

Good, child. Now move on to your next question.

Thanks. Okay here it goes. Why should I, and why do I feel bad most of the time when and if I do not give some small change to a beggar that asks me for it on the street? And why sometimes do I still feel bad after giving? Why do I have that feeling of guilt and shame to myself? And what should I do, Parent?

33

Good question. This one is an interesting one, so I will explain it in a more subtle way. Now I say this to you child: You are here to live your dream, and this is your dream. You my child, do not like and enjoy giving money to beggars on the streets because you do not receive anything from them that fulfills who you are in your dream of reality in the moment. You instead rather give it to someone, whom you know, in that it will return the same way you gave or some other form of sort, to help you when you need it in your dreams.

You want to give money only when it achieves a certain obviously expected outcome of fulfillment or reciprocated compensation. Therefore this means that, it is difficult for you to give or handout money justly, when clearly in doubt of its use, to whom you give it to. You create thoughts and ideas of what will happen with that money, and what will that person do with it. Will they do as they say, or are they just taking you for a nice short ride until you disappear on that corner, and then think of you stupid for actually believing them?!

Yes, that is true Parent. I mean even when I am at my lowest, and I know that I do not have enough. But when a good close person that I know, asks for help with some cash of sort, I am willing to sacrifice. I do this, because I know I will get my money back, and I believe that it is going for a good reasonable course, and if that is no main concern, then I know that I can ask for a favor at some time to compensate. Yet on the other hand, even at my lowest, I feel not to sacrifice for a lone vagrant beggar on the street, because I know if I give, that he or she will keep on asking for it, and therefore thus gives nothing back, in the process of to where I want to be in my dream but rather keeps on taking.

Yes, that is exactly what you do and, think, child.

Be present, my good child. Now listen to this; that feeling of bad, guilt, shame and sadness that you have when you do not give, arises because you think, and put yourself in that position of that person who is asking as a vagrant on the street—that is to say if ever it was you. You feel guilty because you yourself would expect to be given at least something when you ask for it, especially when you do not have. And remember that for you to find yourself in an asking position, and begging for money, is because you are not clear and sure of yourself of what you can really do. If you were sure, then you would be assured to have money all the time, by yourself, by doing what you love, and that is to say by displaying and giving your skills talentedly majestic as you are.

Now you should also be aware of this. That feeling of rueful sadness that you have, when you do decide to give something to a beggar on the streets, arises because you have plans for that which you are giving away, in your dreams. It feels sad, because you have taken something away from yourself, to give it to someone who will not give back to you, instead of yourself, by giving it to someone that will give you something that you want, need and would like to have in return for compensation now or later, in this life.

Wow, I got that one as well, Parent. Thanks.
You are welcome, child.

So let me get this, Parent. Are you saying that I should not beg for money?

This is what I am saying, child. Choose whatever you may choose, yet be sure that it is what defines you as who you truly are in this moment for this particular course of being and living, in your dream to your value. Should you choose to be and continue begging, see and be aware by realizing the amount of value of worth you are placing on yourself, by loving to gain money from people on the streets, instead of loving and valuing the worth of your skills of talent in your dream to gain money.

Okay ⋯ thank you Parent, I understand.

It is again, my pleasure, sweet one.

Now, listen to this. Whenever you will, do, be, and are experiencing poverty on the streets as a homeless person it is because of circumstances of events influencing your choice, yet not making a decision for you. With this truth, you should understand and accept that, your situation and condition of experiencing is of your highest stigmatic choice in the moment. This simply means that life on the streets is not a coincident. Nothing ever happens by coincident or chance, yet rather, but, by choice. Now, here is a terrifying truth about you. When living on the streets, you reject the offer of leaving or changing your life from it, by refusing to use the opportunity around you.

Okay, that's interesting. How do I do that ⋯ I mean what causes me to do that?

Now, because this is your dream, and everything is possible in a dream. You have placed opportunities very close to near, around you, so that you may use them, to get out of a situation whenever you are ready and have decided to. When on the streets, all you do is beg and ask for something, from people you meet or passing. Each and every single day that passes, you always end up having received something in your hands, which in most cases is money. Yet with this every day privilege, you do not set goals or things to achieve. For instance: an idea of saving that money for better good of self is let slip and regarded as futile when it comes to mind, only because of thinking that, what you have is not enough, and that it seems and sounds crazily ridiculous to have this idea, considering where you are. Even though you have been receiving it for the past five or ten years, you would choose not to save or use it on your dream. Why? I tell you this, only because you are regarding what you have as less. When you really wish, desire and want to leave the streets for better, you would stand up, and say, "now it is enough!" You would tell yourself that, you do not value your condition, therefore thus accumulate what is given out of love by the next person, to use it for better and good of what you think you deserve.

Mm ⋯ I hear that. I understand, Parent.
Good, very good, sweet one.

Mm ⋯ hum ⋯ so now, what should I do when asked for money, Parent?

Only do what pleases you. Yet do not be hard on yourself for not giving, child. I mean there is no point, when especially what you give creates sad emotion of feeling and does not come back when you desire it to. It makes no sense running your pockets, wallet and or bank account dry, and then be sulky, rueful, sadly bitter and angry about it. Do choose not to give to gain misery but, rather joy. Do choose to not give yourself unpleasant moments and circumstances, when you do not want.

Yet I tell you this, you should understand the experience chosen by that person on the streets begging. The boldness, bravery and willing power to experience what you say, "I cannot live like that" on the streets—out of their love. Praise them, be kind and respect them, yet do not condone and encourage them to remain the same. Tell them that, yes, they have done it, and that they can choose differently for there are other pleasures than that, yet only as they wish, again. Be the inspiration. Do choose not to look down on them, because now, you understand why and how they are experiencing what they are now.

Oh my only lovely good one, I am sharing this, with you now, because you are the one that can make the suffering of the poor stop. You are the one with riches and wealth, thus it is that I have chosen to engage with. Because with you, I know that the world is in safe hands for good.

FORGETTING TO REMEMBER KNOWING

This is what love says

Oh my child, my one and only dearest loved child. The one I proclaim profoundly to heart. The one who is beautiful in all-ways as creation itself by itself! You are the great wise that knows everything, the one that creates and destruct eternally to perfect wisdom of self. Your wisdom of knowledge is unparalleled to a significant sheer degree of greater magnitude. Oh my sweet hearted child that is uniquely precious such as a protea flower that grows on the mountain covered with hazy cloth of mist—of the cape facing the ever flowing ocean deep. The one that is—oh yes you are the great wise one in true nature. You are wisdom, child!

So from that piece that you just recited, I would assume that you intend to mean that I am wise and that I know everything?

I tell you this, I know and I am clear of this, that you do know everything child.

Well you do know that, that is hard to believe right? Oh how I wish I did know everything, Parent.

Well not for me because I already believe because I am as I know ⋯ but for you yes, I do understand from where you are, and that is why I am here with you again to guide you through to ultimate understanding of yourself.

I am interested, so please ⋯

Now listen with your heart and be present with soul, be in the moment for what I am to say is your truth. I am here right where you are now, to remind you how you forget in order to remember knowing. I tell you this: no soul is stupid even in its physical form child. Therefore this means that no one is stupid. There is not a single soul being that is stupid in all of creation in the entire universe. Stupidity does not exist.

Wait, you just wait a minute here! Are you saying that there is no such thing as a stupid person? Are you saying that everybody is smart and intelligent?

Well not much of a person but a soul being (in any body it occupies), child. Yet in your case, yes there is no such thing as a stupid person.

Well I am sorry, but I have been around and I have seen stuff, I have seen a lot of stupid and goofy things done by stupid people. I mean a person can really get mindless hey! And I will be like, "seriously! Like really now, who does that?!" And also I have seen people failing to understand simple things such as math of 1 + 1, (just to exasperate and exaggerate there), or a simple subject in school and cannot even read or write their name in this day-and-age of modern time. I have seen people get drunk that they even struggle to walk and retain balance. So please, enlighten me to your believe of understanding, Parent!

Wow, look and listen to you! You really can put up a show if you want hey!

Yah I know, I get like that sometimes, Parent. You should put me on stage and see me in action performing. My good friend you will be amazed, staggered and regaled because I am like: 'Hey, hey, get down, back up and break a leg. Shake it ⋯ shake it ⋯ hey! To the left and to the right, and take it off. Oh yeah!' You know what I mean?

I think I do. Now that was very entertaining child, well done! Would you like an Oscar or a Grammy for that?

Nah, I think we should get back to more serious stuff before we get carried away.

Okay good. Now sit properly so that you can pay attention.
Okay I am good and ready.

No I am serious, I can see you ⋯ now sit comfortably and properly, child.
Okay ⋯ okay, jeez just relax, I am sitting properly.

Good.

You are a genius in wisdom. Yes child, I tell you this; one of few many difficult things to do is to forget. And also one of many few very easy and simplest things to do is to forget. As much difficult it is to forget, it is very easy to forget because you do it every moment, second, day and time intuitively spontaneously in knowledge of it.

I am not sure if I understand that, Parent.

I know child because I understand, and as you know me, I will cause you to understand and know.

I say this child: You struggle to forget who you are now. By this I mean that it is difficult for you to forget the person you are right now concerning your current suffering and struggling conditional-situation of erratic emotions or lack—for your own good, as so you may remember who you honestly truly are in your ultimate dream of whom and where you would choose to be in life. You complain, whine and cry out loud because of and in your suffering of not living your dreams fully. You say this thing called life is difficult and not simple or easy because you are not living the dream you should have and deserve. You even say it is not working, no matter how much or hard you try, this thing called life just does not work! And I tell you this, oh yes it does work because I made it work! I made it work because I only remembered what made and is making it work so it may work. The irony is that you are my fair equal, and this means that you are also just as capable of making life work just as much as I have, and am. And now I say this to you, when you really think, feel and know that what you are doing or being in life is difficult, not easy and not working towards where you should be in life of your true dream, then you should choose to forget about it. Yes I am saying exactly that, just forget about it. Forget what you are doing and only remember who you think you are in your dream.

Now listen, be very present, for I am to explain the great mystery of knowledge. This is the parallel paradox of wisdom. This is what confuses, and causes you to undermine your true potential of knowing everything as wise as you are. This is forgetting to remember knowing. Therefore listen, because this is how you do it.

To forget is to ignore. And to ignore is to willingly think and pretend, and act as if a certain particular thing does not exist in experience, within or at any exact instant moment by not considering it. And what you choose not to exist or experience, is what you think is not important within or at that exact instant moment by not considering it, in favor for what you like and desire in that very same moment. In simple terms, to forget is to think about a different particular thing that you desire over any, for as long or as briefly short as you can, in this moment, by regarding others less. Forgetting does not mean inexistence or inexperience of something else. It is simply the willing pretentious act of ignorance towards a thing by not thinking of it or looking at it, at any moment, for a different desired other.

Okay I hear you, Parent. So are you saying that everything exists and is experienced, and that I am simply ignorant towards some things because I do not want or wish to see or experience them at this moment, for something I like and desire at this moment?

Yes, child, that is exactly what I am saying.

Forgetting is caused and manifested to reality, by focusing and concentrating perceived attentive energy towards a desired specific particular thing or object of matter in ignorance of others. Once energy is focused and concentrated, it channels and creates to form the realized object into being from your perspective of conscious, in which the energy has clustered itself miscellaneously in sight. Now, in this process of concentration and creation on a particular object, other already formed objects of reality, still respectively and singularly continue on having their current form and motive of intend, whether in motion or not, at a point in space. This simply means that, when you focus and pay attention to and on one or other few things, other things of matter proceed doing what they are intended to do, in any point in space in your dream of where you want to be, currently right now.

Okay ⋯ yah I hear you, but now tell me, how come and why do I forget most of the time? I mean, I would put something here, and forget that I had placed it right there, and search for it for a while. I would put keys, money or some particular small valuable in my left front pocket and, then look and feel for it in my right or back pockets, where I did not put it! Why is that and why is it like that most of the time, Parent?

Good question! You are so brilliant that you only have good thoughts and questions, thus you have asked a good question for its enlightenment, and that is how intelligent you are. Therefore you are doing good!

Now to your question; the reason why you do forget at most, if not many times where you put and leave things, is because you do not station that particular thing or item in one place.

Yah I know that, Parent—

Wait ... I am still saying. Now, your memory records all that is, which is what you create to existence. So whatever you do you should know that it is recorded, (as you already do know this by now). Now, when you put a particular thing anywhere somewhere, and you forget, and look for it anywhere somewhere else other than where you put it. It is because your memory searches all the places that it remembers, of that particular desired thing being once at. You would put something here, and then move or put it somewhere over there. And if that is not all, the following day you would put it on or at a different place entirely from before. Today your small valuable is in your front right pocket, the next moment in your left pocket, and then again, tomorrow in your back pocket. With all the shifting and moving of things to different places all the time, your memory records all of these things, events and places they are at. Hence you look for it where it once was at some moment of time ago, where you put it before.

Wow ⋯ okay I see, Parent.

Now, depending on how fast or quick your memory serves you as you think (progressively), it would go through all the possible places a particular thing is situated very quick within seconds, and locate it directly where it is without guessing or assuming the others, yet still going through them. Things that are always stationed in, on or at one place are not, most of the time easily forgotten, because they do not move around about.

Alright, I got that as well, Parent. So now tell me, are you suggesting that if I do not want to forget I should keep and place things always all the time in, on or at one place?

Now that would be best for you, yet I am not telling you to do that. I am showing, explaining and making you realize how you forget and what happens when you do forget and how you can prevent and manipulate it for your own good so that you may know by remembering.

Okay ⋯ I got that.

Now also, for you to be able to remember a thing, by willing, you would have to choose to be more observant, focused and aware of it, and where it is placed. This means that, whether you are placing, throwing or tossing something somewhere on to a place, you would have to be very observant, considerate and aware of where it is put or placed, child. Once a thing is always there, it is not forgotten where it is, because it is always there! You know where your home or house is at, because it has never moved from there since it was built. You do not leave a house, and then come back to find it somewhere else ⋯ and then act surprised by saying, "where did it go? It was just right there, I mean, I know that I left it there." as you would with your keys or anything else for that matter, that you always move and shift around, and even lose.

Mm ⋯ hah, it's funny that you actually had to use a house there as an example.

I have to make you understand, good one. You will understand this forgetfulness and remembering of things to know, when we get to dreams, because you forget out of choice and from love.

I can' t wait to get to dreams, parent. Sounds like it is going to be epic and interesting!

It is already interesting now, child.

Now listen again: Remembering is to connect the reality of events. To remember something, is to think now, and recreate it, whether differently or similarly the past occurred event. To connect something, is to follow and add links of occurred events as you progressively think by going through them, to make a choice. To think is to make a choice from options—that are already available as you create. Whatever you remember is and can be redone for its desired purposeful experience.

Wow ··· okay, I see. So you also mean that, for me to be able to remember something, I can do it the same way as before, or I can do it differently? So it actually matters not of how I go about it, as long as the desired outcome result is met, then it is good, Parent?

Yes, child. Remembering therefore is a link of motion that moves through space, and connects forgotten events to know them again. This explicit rationality therefore means that there is only existence; and it can be forgotten, as in when ignored, by will.

Now knowing is to remember what you have forgotten from your experiences. Whatever it is that you know, it is because of the love of experience for it as many times as you can, by remembering the experience practically. And whatever you forget, it is of less interest and pleasure, no matter how important it was before, in that moment of letting go. Yes child, because of the love of receiving certain desired pleasure, you have thus have had your experience of it. Therefore knowing is re-experiencing existence by remembering, (particularly what you have forgotten from your ignorance), by will, as many times as you may desirably wish, just like every second or day.

45

Wait ⋯ hold it again! Oaky I understand knowing what I have forgotten and have experienced. But now tell me, how can I know what I have not experienced and done?

You see, exactly my point. You have ignored the true existing fact, that I have mentioned to you, and thus have you forgotten what I said, and what you also asked! This is what I said: 'Forgetting does not mean inexistence or inexperience, it is simply the willing pretentious act of ignorance towards a thing by not thinking of it or looking at it, at that moment, for a different desired other.' And this is what you asked: "So are you saying that everything exists and is experienced, and that I am simply ignorant towards some things at this moment, for something I like and desire at this moment?" , and I greed with you, child.

Ah ⋯ oh ⋯ yah I remember that.

Yes, you do because you have done it before, but just simply ignored it by not thinking and considering it, in this or at that now moment. And this is what I meant, when I said that, 'one of few many difficult things to do is to forget. And also one of many few very easy and simplest things to do is to forget. As much difficult it is to forget, it is very easy to forget because you do it every moment, second, day and time intuitively spontaneously in knowledge.' And this is to say that, in its existence. You quickly and easily forget things now, and you also quickly remember things now, to know them again as you did before from your forgotten ignorance. There is nothing that you do not know, yet only have forgotten it, and thus think that it is your first encounter and experience of it over a long due span of moment being held. This means that you have experienced, and are experiencing everything now. And now I tell you again, child. Whatever it is that does not produce desired outcomes in your dream, just forget about it, and remember whatever works as you create it anew.

Oh how beautiful it is child—just the way it is. Now listen to this for I am saying it. The reason you have asked yourself these questions of (why, what, how and or when), which in this case is: "why" is it taking long for my life to work? "What" should I do to make it work? "How" should I make it work? And finally you say "when" is it going to work? And this is what I will tell you my good lovely sweet child. Your life has never not worked. Your life has perfectly worked just the way you have decisively chosen it to be and intended ⋯ please let me finish before you ask what exactly am I trying to say or getting at here.

Okay you got me there Parent.

So ⋯ this is my answer to your questions. You have decisively and willingly chosen the cyclic routine of few of many more divine universal truths and things to do. There are a lot of things to do in the universe, yet you have decisively chosen to settle for only just a few past experiences repetitively in your life that you love. You have and still are living your past experiences almost every day if not every month or year. Instead of living through being the cause of the experienced moment, you have and are still living it through for the experienced moment to be the cause and course of your life. And I do know that you do not understand what I have just said.

Yes ⋯ I really do not understand, Parent.
It is all good, child, I will make it simple for you.

Child, to you that will and still thinks that sexual intercourse is good and pleasurable, for how long will you think it so?
Hum ⋯ I am not sure. I guess as many times and as long as I will.

Good. Child, to you that knows, has, have and will again intercourse sexually pleasurable and good, for how long will you do so?
Hum ⋯ I am not sure. I guess as long and as many times as I will.

Good. Child, the one that has, still is and will again eat food and drink water, for how long will you do so?

Hum ⋯ I am not sure. Again, I guess as many times as I will.

Good. Child, the one that will and thinks work is good—and is still working, for how long will you do and think it so?

Hum ⋯ I am not sure. I guess as long and as many times as I will, until I think it is not.

Good. Very good you have done. Well that just summarizes everything then.

Well, I guess it does, Parent.

You see child, this is exactly what I mean. Just as you will and have chosen to have sex, babies, food, to go work, do and enjoy sport. To drive in a car, bike or fly a plane, to pray, party, fight, to kill, or go to war daily, weekly, monthly and or annually, and to take it a bit farther we can say in a decade, century and or a millennia. It is the same dream that of your grater past. Great thousands of years ago, you enjoyed war and the killing of any being. You enjoyed sex, food, work and power by subjugation. With all of that having been said, great thousands of years of the very same thousands after, you still have not progressed that much, because you love this dream of your past thus you keep reliving it. Now to make all of this to stop, you would have to choose to forget about it, and this is one thing you are not ready for at this soon moment.

Okay ⋯ I hear you loud and clear. You are going all the way through to me. Man I would hate to remember all the nasty and bad things I did in the past.

Yes, exactly! This is the exact cause, because you so much love and hate some of the things that you did in your past, as in that, you love to hate what you did in the past, (you have created a new life), hence thus as such you have forgotten all about it, by ignoring and pretentiously acting as if it is not there,

48

and has not ever happened and that it does not exist. It is love, your love that creates your experiences. You love where you are right now, thus as such you are experiencing your love. Love is dream making, and you love making dreams, child.

Wow, great, Parent! So I am supposed to take all of that in without even digesting it, and just swallow it. Well it's a bit hard to swallow I must say ⋯ phew!

Yes, child. If your work does not produce your desire, then you should choose to forget about it, and choose to remember what produces your desires. Just remember what is working!

Yeah ⋯ nah ⋯ no, I think I got it.
Good, very good!

Now tell me, Parent. Why have I wasted or gone to school if I have known everything all along? And is school necessary by all means, since I know everything and I am wise as you say and claim me to be? Do I need education because I am all knowing and wise?

Good, very good you are doing. Now I tell you this: like I have said before, you are created and are born as birthed, smart and intellectually creatively intelligent by knowing everything and being wise. You are never created stupid and not knowing. No creation creates the unknown. Now first, you have gone to school because you thought as you still do think now, that you do not know a certain particular thing. You went to school because you thought you did not know how to talk and speak and write properly, even though you could, (only to find out that now you can, and are able to). Yet no school teaches you how to talk because you observe and absorb speech and reflected it out by perfecting it the way you already know how from the world around you.

You have seen your parent and people close around you, and everybody in your surroundings, walking, and are thus inspired to walk as they do, by pushing, thriving and driving yourself from within with strength and force of your own will-might, the way you already know how to do.

Yes, isn't that learning, Parent? I mean I learn by looking at how something is done from others and then I do it the way I see it.

Yes, child, that is why you have to see it first, as so to be it. Whatever it is that you see, you can as you will, be it by doing it as liked. When something appears in your mind, by imagining it, you see it and are then able to create or bring it forth, just as you would when you search for an answer in your head from mind. If you do not see anything or something, you cannot be it because it is not there as you do not see it as an image, and cannot identify it. Yet you have seen everything and just only choosing to experience what you have observed by far, your deepest loved desire from your sight in your dream by forgetting the others in ignorance, as if they do not exist.

Okay, I see what you mean.

Now listen, my sweet lovely one and only child—the one that I pride myself with gladness and hold close to heart. No one or anything has taught you. You have only observed how a particular thing is done and have chosen to do or be it by choice as so you remember and love, from liking it and allowing yourself to follow its regulatory pattern, and then perfect it to specification.

Now, knowing is simply knowing and, being is simply being. You can and may know something and not be it by choice. Also you can as you may, know something and be it as you choose it, only by great desire for it. Now at this moment, you know numbers of mathematics to a certain level of degree, yet you have chosen not to extend, expand and perfect it greater, by enhancing beyond your current understanding and knowledge of numbers, because you are choosing to be great at something different that interests you more, and that you love and desire. And there is more of math than what your knowledge possess in creation right now.

This simply means that you may know and understand something and not indulge in it or be it, and yet this does not mean that you do not know what it is. The more you stay out of tune and practice of what you know by stopping doing it, by ignoring it for something else other of interest to your like, in this moment, is the more you forget how to do and create it. Yet deep in your heart and consciousness it is saved, you know that it can be done again by you, only if you would and choose to remind yourself, and that it does exist. Being on the other hand, is just simply having to settle for any state or part of knowledge that you choose from all existing knowledge in its categories.

Okay, I got that one as well, Parent.
Good, very good.

Now here is your truth. Because of that you are so wise, a genius and so intelligent. You only go to school to offer your ability of understanding that you have already of things and knowledge, for recognition and approval beyond yourself.

I am sorry, what, recognition beyond myself? Hum ⋯ please, Parent⋯

Yes, recognition beyond yourself. This simply means that you are able to understand what you greatly choose, and also along with that ability, you choose to want what you know, to be accepted, recognized and approved on a larger broaden scale beyond yourself by other people. With this truth, again, it means that you place yourself in a position of not knowing what you can understand, only by will, to be that which you call a clueless, dumb or stupid person—(as you prefer naming).

Now, since you consider and regard yourself as not knowing, you then such as thus as you say and think, go to school to learn or understand or remember, without knowing what you are going to learn or be in this life, towards your dream. You do this by ignoring. You venture to an institution having knowing what is there, yet not having made a choice of what or who to be from the pool of knowledge that you possess.

So you mean that I go to school because I do not know who I want to be, yet I know who I can be and what to know, Parent?

You go to school because you have not made and, are still making a choice of who you really want to be in this life (yet within in the borders of school), as to be recognized for it, in the process of showing your ability of understanding towards what you will make a choice of, in your dream. Had you already remembered and known, in decision of it, you would be it and only teach it by showing it.

Wow, okay, that makes sense, Parent.

Now listen oh great wise one. This is what school is for. School is for only a moment and time when you say and think that you do not know. It is there to offer and give a reminding option of choices of who you really desire to be. It is within the school borders that you get to choose as you have forgotten, to be: a scientist, mathematician, artist, preacher, philosopher, psychologist, athlete or a sports person, an educator, business person, a machine or device operator and etc. School is, at most times, where you are exposed to a variety of resources that assist and help to continue your understanding of knowledge of things that you already know, of which you have forgotten from your past. It is within this institutional structure that, those of old from past in the present moment of time, that with their knowledge, have decided to organize and carry forth what you particularly seek to remember as it already exists.

Now, listen to this, for it is your wisdom. Remember I said that 'you only go to school to offer your ability of understanding that you have already of things and knowledge, for recognition and approval beyond yourself' ?

Yes, I do good Parent.

Good. Now listen then, for this is what is. In same relative truth, you go to school to improve its knowledge base and understanding by offering it. You are the one with great wisdom oh good child, yet, as we have said before many a time, you have forgotten.

When you are in school, information that is brought to you through learning is of old. This means that you learn old past information from generations before you, therefore meaning that you learn nothing new. Now, bearing this great truth in mind, you then attend the institution to understand this old information. Because you have such great magnificent understanding and intelligent wisdom, once having it understood and known to you, you then thus clearly see, and as it is apparent right now, that there are things that can be done to improve and better education for yourself now, and for posterity and the generation to come then. Thus as such that it is that you work hard in school to solve old problems for new. These improvements come to you as ideas because you know and have had them all along—your very own ideas that exist already (from your memory), of which you create and label as invention, innovation, amendments and creativity.

After having an idea, you then pass it over for approval because you are quite ambivalent about yourself, of which it is then used generally by the social public outside the premises of school. You do this, and the school allows you to, because it constantly seeks your ideas to move forward and experience new things, within itself and in the world at large in general. Because when a system, (and that is to say information), does not change, then that means there would be no improvement or progress to and from the old generation

53

nor to the new, and that the same tools will be used and the same experience will be had as many times until there comes a time that the great new, such as you, come with new ideas that they have from their knowledge and understanding of what should work better for them.

I tell you this, my great intelligent one. No building of institute produces a great student or learner. It is the learner or student that produces great institutions. You can as you may, go to any institution that offers high quality education beyond any standard measure. Yet when you do not understand the teachings, and are not passing, the school fails with you. And the more of those who do not understand, the more the whole school does not understand.

Your failure on a subject or class is because of less interest in it, and you just want to ignore and forget it in your reality by not knowing it as to not have its experiences. And yet even when you do enjoy school, it is because you have fun with others, meaning that you enjoy the playfulness, entertainment and fun things with other learners by just being yourself. And when the time to focus on books and learn comes, your interest tends to dissipate. And yet also when you have fully decided to concentrate and pass, you are only doing it to prove and show others that you also can, when and if you only want (by your highest choice). And that you are just the same as they are, just to fit in, even if you do not want to do it. And finally when you pass something with distinction, it is because you really are enjoying it for the love of it, and it seems effortless for you because you are only concentrating on it—as it is your love. This truth firmly and clearly states that you make education, most importantly of who you are! (Your own education). Yet what you love and who you are, is everywhere and not only in school. You are indeed intelligent.

Knowledge of wisdom is everywhere. Each and every single second possess great wisdom. Therefore the most important thing to master and pass is your life. And every day as you wake up, you are presented (as you have before, and now), with a great opportunity to perfect yourself and get yourself right no matter how long, and how many times it takes you, to finally understand who you are. Therefor this means that you cannot and will not fail. This truth eliminates the thought that you have of thinking that you only pass when you are at school. Yet life itself is more than school and you are made of it. There is no need for school for you are already in the holy moment of wisdom per second right now. Life is full knowledge and does need education. The only thing that you already have right now with you, is to remember that one great thing of many, about yourself that you so much love, and be it by choosing.

Oh great wise one, listen to the gentle echoes of knowledge passing to mind. Be here with full intelligence as you are. At the moment contrary to your truth of wisdom, you have lately in your life chosen to accept and believe that you should attend school under the idea that you need money in order to be who you are, whether rich or to live. And the only way to do this is to have qualified academia education.

You do this, as to be able to participate into the games and reality of the monetary system that is approved by the great masses in general beyond yourself, in this world. Because even though you might know something and are good at it, yet it is difficult to enter the game system of monetary, as you like and love to choose to, because they or it requires approval and recognition that you can do it. I tell you this, yet this does not mean that you cannot do it without anyone's or its approval.

The most grandest approval of all, is of self. Once and when you do approve yourself that you are capable of doing something, and that you are qualified by recognizing your value of worth and who you are; you will do it with excellence. At this moment in life, you have not approved yourself from within of what you can do, beyond and despite of what others think you cannot do. Having set this self-limitation and waiting, you have thus let many opportunities pass you by, because you think you are not qualified and are not ready on the scope of written document of paper by someone. This form of thinking and believe has thus made you less rich, concerning paper money or digital. Having believed that you cannot, and that you are not rich, you have then ventured in school to attain papers, as so to have more riches of paper. In the process of all of this, moments of self-enjoyment of who you are pass by. The things that you mean for yourself to do as young, you then do when old. Now I tell you this special one, choose you. Choose your dream of desire before any education, and its education will choose and show you money of wealth and even more than that, that you desire for now above most all.

I tell you this, oh great wise one. Having no qualification of paper of approval, does not mean or make you stupid and poor. Intelligence is the ability to create without fooling different. This means that it is to create something that does or works accordingly as intended by you, and not false as to impress, without functioning. When something is created with and by false impressions, it determines your own level of thinking; which is that, you make something specially to work differently as declared. This is to say that when you make a particular thing, and even say by declaring it that it is to or, for one particular purpose, yet deep in your thought you know that you created and made it for the other result, then you are fooling yourself, because you already know how it will turn out to be. You already know the result of the outcome.

To create something to fool someone, shows that you are capable of thinking foolishly and then believe that you are actually impressively intelligent to make someone, something or people believe that!—Yet you are the first fool to believe that it will work! You literally fool yourself first, before others.

Now, poverty exists accordingly to your intelligence of undesired and unpleasant situations of lack. Therefore since that all souls of being possesses intelligence, they do not need papers of approval, because their imagination creates intelligently for their experiential events to exist, even to believe that they are poor in the universe, when they are not. Therefor the very sets of creativeness and imagination you would use to get qualified on paper, you should choose to use them on what you really love, using your skills of talent magnificently and majestically in your daily-second of life; then shall you see what power you possess from within without any statement of paper when you approve it yourself to be!

Wow, mm. I am learning a lot here, Parent. This is a revelation that clears and opens my eyes, for I never think in this manner.

Forgetting is a choice whether subliminal, subconscious, conscious or unconscious. The relationship of forgetting to remember knowing is significantly sheer, and should be used for great experiences of thought. Therefor true wisdom is manipulated adjustably for outcomes of known results. This is to say that when you feel and think by knowing that you are suffering, struggling and or not coping in any situations that you have chosen, you should simply forget that horrible experience by ignoring it for something better pleasing. In doing this you then focus on what is important as you remember by thinking. Once having forgotten your past, and have remembered a great idea of and about yourself, you then know what to do and thus become the result of what you know.

Wisdom is to remember good loving things, by doing them as you think to be. And so far, this is as far as you have allowed your wisdom to be, and you can as you may by will, take it elsewhere further you think is more better. I tell you this: it is that simple, and that easy. Just forget, remember, and know. Yet choose wisely as you are—(in the process of it), because you know and you can only when you will, be whatever it is you choose.

Mm ⋯ okay. Okay ⋯ I think I got it Parent.
Good. Very good oh wise one.

DEATH OF FEAR

This is what love says

Oh my sweet child—my beautiful baby. You are brave, bold and courageous, and there is not any other like you. You my one and only child do not fear death. Yes you are resolute and daring towards death. Oh my child, I have sweet fruitful tears that fills me with joyful love because, you have chosen to die for what you believe in. You have stood against all odds of self-destruction towards the body, and you have survived and are still alive because you have lived through them all. And I tell you this, I admire and love you child for your audacious valour.

Now I say and tell you this: death is not painful at all. The phase of dying is beautiful, magnificent and majestically awesome by highest of lowest degree. You shall will to never feel pain when going through the stage of dying. Dying is painlessly great and enjoyable, child.

What do you mean that death is not painful and that it is enjoyable, Parent? Well, I am sorry but I have heard and seen people die in pain—in hideous car accidents and fights, and it is not a good sight!

Well I tell you this: you are living through pain right now—emotionally and physically. You wound and injure your body playfully and carelessly through living and yet you are still alive. You fight others with hands, knives and guns and yet you still survive and are alive to tell. I tell you this, if you can survive bullets and knife wounds through living, you can survive them through dying. The same way you heal and restore yourself inflicted wounds through living as to not feel pain anymore as many times as your physical body and feelings can and has, is the same way you heal yourself through dying as to not feel pain utterly at all, child.

But Parent, a person does and can feel pain when stabbed on the chest deep through to the heart before they die. People do die in pain ⋯

I tell you this, yes you are right. When you are stabbed before you die, you will feel pain because you will be alive at that moment of being stabbed before you pass on. Pain is experienced through living as you now know it, yet pain is not experienced through the transitional process of death as you do not know it and remember. And I am here to assure you that knowledge of remembrance. When your breath leaves your body, it does so painlessly, harmless and, is such a wonderful great feeling of the now wholly holy present moment—it is a total rapture.

I tell you this child, just like as it is beautiful in the moment of life, it is just as greatly beautiful in the moment of death. Look how beautiful it is now, look around you and make a judgment of it. When you see ugly around you, then it is beautifully ugly and that is why you have chosen it. Should it be so that you only see beauty, it is because you have chosen not to label it ugly.

Wait ⋯ but you just wait a minute here. May you explain more on what you mean by that I do not fear death? Are you saying that I can choose to die right now and not be scared and feel no pain at all? What are you saying exactly?

Well I tell you this, this is what I am saying child: Yes you can will to die now, if and when you want choose, and feel no pain anywhere at all.

Nope, no ways, no, no, no! Just imagine dying without pain, please do not fool me.

Yes, you have it! That is exactly what you should do, all you have to do is to imagine. Remember that to create the experience of something or a thing (in you reality), you have to constructively imagine it so that it may be as you remember. And I tell you this, I only will not to fool you, for to fool you is willing to fool myself that I have fooled you, and I am not willing to do that my good friendly child. I tell you this; you do die without pain. All soul beings of the human race and all people do experience death painlessly.

I do hear you, but make me understand fully and completely.
Thank you for allowing me my very good child.

Now listen with your heart, be present with and in soul. Love is dreams and dreams are love, and this is your dream. As long as you are in this form, as long as you are human you will to feel pain. My beautiful child, do not confuse the experiences of living with dying. Dying as you now know and call it, is the process of soul breath leaving the human body for good and not for bad.

Wait ⋯ I have to interrupt you here again, Parent. When you say that— "you will to feel pain" , are you actually saying that I can live now without feeling pain at all by not willing it? Are you saying that I can live without any pain, and also I can die without any pain by not willing it? And these are both achievable on possibility?

Yes!

You know what? You actually stagger me, Parent. You come up with these crazy insane self-acclaimed ideological-ethic concepts beyond orthodoxy, and you think life is easy. I have listened and heard you very clearly on so many occasions. You always say and think that there is nothing out there that cannot not be achieved. You say nothing is impossible and that I am limitless, and now you are telling me that I can live my life without any pain at all whether it is emotional or physical. You stand invisibly boldly before my presence and tell me that death and living wills to be, can, and is pain free. Well I am sorry Parent, you will have to work more harder than you have ever done!

Hum ⋯ oh my sweet child, you of all should know that I have done it all and have been all of it. And now I tell you this, I do not even need to work harder on convincing you because there is nothing hard for me!

Okay then, let me hear you talk your way out of this one.
Thank you for allowing me again, child.

Now listen. Yes you can live your life now without any emotional or physical pain—

How do I do that?

Wait ⋯ let I finish first.
Okay ⋯ okay, sorry. Please enlighten me.

Good, very good. Now I tell you this, yes it has as it is, can and will be done, and with no buts take more than just you. In order to have and live this wonderful life, you would have to first understand the beautiful imaginative creation of it. Once having understood, you should choose to agree with it. And I promise you this, once you have imagined it to creation, understood the creation, chosen and agreed with it, you will love it because it is beautiful indeed.

Now this is what I mean: For you to live this pain free life you would have to agree to it, and not refuse or say no thank you to it as to reject, because it is good life. And this is what you should choose: choose not to get involved in arguments or quarrels of negative nature. Choose not to get involved in fights, and also choose not to carry a knife, gun or any weapon or object of sort that intends to harm any soul being in a body or, something, someone or anything. Choose not to get involved in any violent social mass gatherings, whether it may be protest, a march or a strike, yet rather go for the peaceful ones. Choose not to consume any acid, toxic or sharp and solid consumables that harm and destroys body cells, whether it may be liquid or food. By choosing not the above, you will have rejected physical harm which causes pain of and towards the human body and flesh.

And now I tell you this again, you should choose not to get involved in arguments. Whatever it is that you will choose in your life experience as far and as close as your dream is concerned, you should already know by now that you will feel, because you have already felt upset, angry, happy, glad, hatred, joy and—finally the one that sums it all up—and that is love. Oh my sweet child, how many times do you will to be angry, how many times will you allow anger control and fuel you up with rage? So then my child, since you have felt all these emotions already, and have dealt with them knowingly and accordingly suited on many various occasions in your life, you should choose to feel and experience only the ones that you will, as so not to intend to harm your emotional being. By choosing to have harmless emotions, you will have emotional pain free life. It is that easy and simple, child.

Wow, now that is sweet and good to hear Parent. Now tell me this, say that I do act out and choose to do and be what you have suggested; say that I fully agree and will to be what you say I should choose to be or do. What will happen if someone else other than me creates and desires to attack me from motives of robbing me, because of something that he or she thinks is valuable to them in need of it? What will happen when I am victimized of rape? What should I do in such situations, should I not also have something or anything to defend myself with to fight back? What should I do when a person is just of any cause angry and decides to take it all out on me? How should I react to such situations?

First and far most, good point you have raised. Secondly, this is about you, this is to help you live a pain free life without harming, wounding your body emotionally or physically. And now I will tell you this: you have just created a thought from your imagination of memory, that you would get robbed. This is what I mean when I say that, do not create such thoughts. You should concentrate oppositely positive that such will not happen, and if by when, you will it not to happen, you will only see what is not happening. You should very creatively will the situation, condition and circumstance in the moment by only seeing people being friendly and kind to you. You should choose to see that first from and out of you, portray and project goodness so it may be as you will it, by giving it to the next person or thing. Also remember this, if and when someone feeds off their emotions towards you, you should choose to say "No thank you, it is not a pleasure," as to reject the feeling that is being fed and directed to you to indulge in it. Be able and will to see, recognize and acknowledge the fed feeling for what it is and see if it is worth any value to you to get worked up over it, child.

Wow, now that was just overwhelmingly breath taking. You know sometimes you just go in with it with full force.

Hum ⋯ Well that is what happens when you ask for it, child.

Oh, really?

Yes child. Now I am sure your head must be a bit exhausted and pounding right now from all of this reading and self-talk. Don't you want to like ⋯ hum—do one of those famous dancing moves of yours. You know the ones that you like to do when you are happy and are sometimes alone (in your room). Come on, give some of that ⋯ ooh, ooh ⋯ huh, huh ⋯ shake, shake and shake it off.

Oh my word, I ⋯ I cannot believe you just said that. You know that I am bit shy hey, Parent?

Well are you now?

You though, you just make me laugh. Do you ever take anything serious?
Tell you what child, how about you grab a drink just to cool yourself off.

Oh yah, and I have a choice of what to drink right?

Oh yes you do child, but just remember if the drink you are having is part of your dream. Will you say thank you to it, and is it a pleasure, does it harm your body emotionally or physically and do you really love it?

Wow, you just had to take it there Parent.
Oops, it got bit serious there, not funny anymore is it now?

No! Okay, I think we should get back to serious stuff now before we get carried away, again, and forget.

I will never forget child, and I will always remind you whenever you do forget.

Thank you, that really means a lot.
It is a real pleasure child.

Now listen because I am telling you this. When I said 'yes it has as it is, can and will be done, and with no buts take more than just you.' I meant that it will take all of you, every single one of you to be this. It will take and have you wholly. Firstly like I said before, you become it, you treat yourself in this manner you are projecting. After you are, you then will to treat the other as you have treated yourself. By and in the moment when you are able to will to feel happiness, joy, gladness, tranquility and calmness with love, then you should choose not to give anger, rage, fury, sadness, hate, confusion, disappointment, doubt and guilt to the other as you have liked, and chosen not to receive it from them. Once you have and will to choose being all of this, you will see the world only for great goodness.

Wow, I think I really do see what you mean, Parent.
Well now that you see it, you know it because it is there as you see it, child.

Okay good. Hum ⋯ you said that I am brave and that I do not fear death, can you explain more on this. I would really love to understand, of how do I not fear death. I mean, I know for fact that I am afraid ⋯ I am seriously scared.

I know! Now then, child, you should choose to pay attention to what follows next.

Now this is what I say. Yes you are brave and fearless. You really do not fear death in its ultimate form, and since you do not fear death, you fear nothing at all. You have shown and proven to yourself that you can self-destruct as many times in different ways as to test thy self repetitively. By this I mean that you do not fear anything at all, child, and that includes death. First, you do something in knowledge and understanding of its outcome. The most common thing that you do, and have done mostly in the previous stages of your life, is fighting.

Even though you fully realize, know and understand that the outcomes of being involved in a fight, are severe and fatal, as such of wounding, injuring and ultimately ceasing the body' s operations to death. You still put that rational fact aside by ignoring it, and engage by encountering your opponent in a fight, to defend yourself whether playfully or by the side of your egotistical honorable reputation of strength and power. At this degree it means that you do not fear the outcomes of what will happen in that active moment, because even though you were afraid at first, yet you faced and challenged a fear that you were scared of, by choosing and willing to be brave and fearless regardless. Therefore this means that you are fearless and brave to any possible outcome—and death itself—of which in the end (for something new)—you are ultimate to choose!

Wow ⋯ now that was some insight, thank you.

It is all good, my good friendly child. Now listen again, fighting is not the only thing you do or have done. Now, as a reminder; first, you do something in knowledge and understanding of its outcome. This means that you simply know what will happen. When you know what will happen, you prevent and avoid some disliked unfavorable outcomes that are in your knowledge base of your understanding. When you prevent and avoid some certain outcomes, it means that you will for them not happen by averting as so not to be experienced. Now in regards to you being involved in a fight, you mostly prevent and avoid being killed or dying, as so not to experience death that is in your knowledge of experience.

Now, you have confused avoidance and prevention, for fear. Avoiding death does not mean fear, rather the power and will to prevent the seen undesired and unfavorable outcome experience as it flashes from the future to the past in your imagination (from your memory), that you know and understand, from happening, and this means that you avert. What you avoid and prevent, can and will be experienced when ultimately decisively ready to be faced and challenged by not being avoided and prevented any more as you have. So far you have experienced, and have eventually ultimately decisively faced and challenged all pain in its forms through your existence by not avoiding and preventing it.

The two forms of pain are emotional and physical. Physical pain is physical pain, whether pinched, cut, stabbed, burnt, or shot— it still feels as pain physically without any difference. The same as to emotional pain: emotional pain is emotional pain, whether rejected, denied, disliked or hated or loathed, it still feels as emotional pain from love without any difference. Now then, until you are ready to experience pain again by challenging and facing it, now in this moment or the next, in any of its form as you have before, you will do so by creating an opportunity for it again. This means that you can and will allow yourself to be in love only to experience hating that person (the pains of love—hate is a feeling and a pain of love), or that person hating you for who and what you do in the relationship—to feel rejection. You allow and embroil yourself by engaging, to help and stop arguments and fights by actually being involved in them in the sense of trying to stop them, yet creating the very opportunity to experience what you are stopping (which is getting in the arguments itself!).

Wow, okay. I see Parent.

Now, yes you are brave indeed. You are so brave that you cross heavy trafficked roads, and set aside the true fact of its danger. Not only do you cross roads, but you also drive in cars on roads fearless of the outcomes and possibilities. You even say, in your own words: "What is the worst that could happen! Whatever happens—happens!" You say this because you are not afraid, and you choose to forget what exists, as in being ignorant. You walk dangerous streets and places at night in fear, yet so brave and daring towards its reality, because of assuring your readiness and accountability to the situation or event of what will happen, in death.

You do dangerous sports and stunts in daring the possibility of injury and death. You fly planes, handle snakes, and swim and sail the deep blue, you do sky diving, bungee jumping, you even desire to be a soldier or a police officer and carry guns to go on a shootout or war to face bullets, if necessary, no matter what the cost, even if it is life. You have unsafe and untested sex with your partners, and you even contemplate on suicide, just as you have done it before in your past existence. You do all these acts of bravery as many times you can to prove to yourself countlessly that you can self-destruct and will to be fearless.

I tell you this, you do not fear to die thus you have and will kill fear by death to live your dream.

Hold it ⋯ just hold it right there. So you are saying that, when I am dead I do not fear anything (and that I may be alive in death), Parent? And it is also part of my dream?

Yes, that is exactly what I am saying. When you are in a state that you call dead, you do not fear anything because at that point you realize that you are still alive, but only just left the body that you know and have spent time in, or with.

Now listen, these are the two things you fear. You fear pain because it is painful, not death. Also you fear because you do not know where you will go when you die, because you forgot, and have not made the decision in this progressive moment to recreate the memory of the experience of how it should be. This is to say that you fear the unknown place, only because you are not clear of where you are after the process of death, because you are ignoring the fact that you will soon die and are pretending as if you are not, thus it is that you are forgetting. You fear this because, from your observation of others, you think that you do not see where the dead go to live.

Of course, Parent, I do not know where the dead go to. Well I know the grave yard ⋯ but I mean I do not know where all dead people passed on are at. If I knew, I would go and fetch the person I love the most, now in this moment, and bring them back, or stay there if it's a good place.

Well, here is something that will shock you, child. The truth is that, you are spending time with the loved dead ones right now in this moment, and you are already dead from life in living, and you know where the dead are. Yes you are dead alive (you are already dead right now!). And with no regret I am terminating this subject. We will have to hold it right here, because you will not understand it as of yet. Yet you will understand it better when I explain dreams to you, child.

Okay ⋯ I will wait.
Good, very good, child.

PRAYER IN MOMENT

This is what love says

Oh my loving child. The one that has fallen on rough flat grounds on knees in moments of desperateness, in agony and cheer of joy for an answer to be produced in fulfillment and achievement. The one that has shed a tear and implored to the open heavens that never shut, within mind with closed eyes. The one that has vented aches of sorrow, shame, forgiveness and guilt from the heart. You are the greatest prayer ever alive to live, that calls forth to manifest the request for desires to be had. You are a true prayer. Oh my perfect one that has approved and disapproved relation of material and action to your dream, in the moment of prayer. You are a prayer in the moment.

Okay, prayer ⋯ a very popular subject on this world. So, what do you have to say and tell me about it, Parent?

Oh yes indeed you are correct. I will tell you what you have done in prayer, and from there, what you do next is all up to you just as it has been your entire life through out to now, by decision.

Okay, I won' t say much as you would expect. So now tell me, what say you, Parent?

Now this is what say I: I tell you this, you have been praying and are still praying right now at this moment as we speak and as you read this, yet you do not see it and have confused prayer to derail, delay and even slow down your requests of the things you desire by praying.

Yep, right ⋯ you know it. This is the time when I have to jump in and interrupt. Wait ⋯ so you are saying that I pray and confuse my prayers by praying, and it slows, delays and derails down the things I request? How can that be, Parent?

Now, be present for this concerns your prayers, therefore choose to be attentive as so you may understand.

I'm ready and all ears.
Good, Child.

Now, know this. Every single thought and wish you make, is your prayer being created. Every single breath and step you make as you take, is your prayer being realized and granted. First and far most of all, you wake every day full of desire. This simply means that, you look forward to a day because there are some things and—so much that you would like and love to do or finish, because you love to, even when feeling down and about at some times. The things that you desire, are the things that which you think about and wish for. You think and wish for these things because you know they exist and are real, hence you pray and ask for them, because you know that you will receive and can have. In your whole entire existence, my lovely good one, you have never prayed for the unknown, because you do not know what the unknown looks like, or what it is.

Now, in order for thoughts and wishes of desire to be met, you breathe and take a step towards them. Having this done, you thus experience the motion of wishful thoughts heading directly in existence already, to you as you move through, as created by you in desire. Hence you find yourself at work, doing and working on the things that you like, love or, did not finish, from the day or days before. Because—number one: you were thinking about it. Two; it exists and is real. Three; you already knew and know that you will end up there, right where you are, now, as you decided before, on each second of

71

moment. To understand this, I therefore tell you this: you do not need, justly as you would choose not to pray sometimes, to pray all the time, because you already are praying all the time, right now.

I am sorry, I missed that, Parent. What?

This is a prayer therefore seek to be attentive soulfully. This is what I say. You do not need to pray because you are already praying. Everything single thing that you do is a prayer and you are moving towards it as it comes to you in reality, because you asked for it, and are willing to wake up and have it in the reality of where you asked for it in your dream of this life. Now, because you already know that the things that you wish, want, like, and love already exists and are real in your world, and that you can have them while you still live here, you do not need to pray for them. All you should choose to do, is to simply say thank you in acknowledgement and understanding of their existence, because you know that you can, may and will to have them, and just go straight to the direction of whatever it is that you want from your desire to attain it.

Wow ⋯ oh, okay ⋯ that' s new. I never thought of it that way, Parent.

I understand my great one and only child. That is why I am here for you, so you may have new thoughts for a greater purpose of less of self, in this moment of feeling slightly happy and full of sadness and alter confusion of giving up in hope for better.

Now listen, fore here is where it is interesting. Once you have prayed, whether by word, deed or thought, you do not have to repeat it again. Because praying again for it, means that it was never granted or heard, according to your blatant expressions and actions of asking again, and that it should be prayed for as many times until it is acquired, when you think so.

72

This form of repetition is a simple mere factor of doubt appearing oblique. This is why you would find a prayer being delayed and taking a long time to approach with parcels of desire, because you keep on praying due to the fact thought that you do not have it yet and, it might not be on the way, thus therefore you feel that you should pray more and more for it, while it is still there and or on the way coming. To have this understood, it simply means that you pray for it some more, even though it is there. This is what I mean when I say that you delay and slow down your prayers. You prayed for this moment to be here and alive on this day, thus you are not praying for or to be alive, but rather most often of many times, are so grateful and glad for the experience of breathing. Because having to pray to live, would simply mean that you are going to, and are dead!

Wow ⋯ I don't know what to say. Hum ⋯ I ⋯ hum ⋯ wow, wow ⋯ phew. Okay.

To understand your prayer better than now, child, you should choose to acknowledge your thoughts to wishes of wants from desire, for your pleasure. Thought is a choice process defining your creation in your dream. Whatever and whenever you think in order to choose, is a moment session of prayer, which means that you are already praying at the instance of it. Once having done with thinking, and have made a choice of want, it then comes to you, and you move to it knowing that it exists, yet first from your thought about it. This is the beautiful moment of granting. It means that it is all yours, just by thought of choice. After this, you are done. Nothing else should be done, only knowing.

You do not need to pray every day, or any other time again, and again for it. All you have to do is to remember it, and continue heading to its direction and claim it. This is why you do get and would receive something you have long ago thought of once, and never expected to have; yet it appears just at the right moment, and you tend to look back in aw because you now remember that you once thought of this—of this beautiful moment only when you remember. And now that it is with you, you will to decide if it is of use now or not, yet you have to know that you asked for it, through thoughts.

Now, therefore with this truth, it means that everything that you do is a prayer; why? Because before you do or take any action, whether spontaneously, randomly or consciously, you think it through first, and this is to say that it is a process through thought for that choice of action you have taken. Now, therefore you should choose to realize every moment of this true beautiful nature that is happening now. Every bite you take, every hand you shake, and every person you meet, and every step and breath you make, you should be aware of what is going on at that moment and, be grateful that it is happening, (now as you think to do it), to be where you are or going, just from a simple thought of needing money. This simply means that you should justly choose to say thank you all the time, because you acquired money from your own efforts in prayer of thought about it daily, to have or buy what you need, child.

Hum ⋯ you just said, "Just from a simple thought of needing money." What do you mean by that, I don't get it, Parent? What does money all of a sudden, have to do with prayer?

This is why, my good child: You are encouraged every day to wake up, by and for money. This happens because you think you do not have enough of it, let alone that sometimes you even think you do not have it at all. Even when you do have enough, you still think that it is not enough to what you value it to. And also by praying more and some more for it, thus because you think (*pray*) you need some more, hence you go every day for some more of what is already, and exists. This is why you have never lacked money.

Wait ⋯ what? Never lacked! Well I am sorry you might just want to rephrase that, Parent.

74

I tell you this, not a week has gone by without you having money. This goes for a month to a year, Child.

Ah ⋯ I got you! Well how about a day then, Parent?
Not even a day, my good child.

Well I don't know about you, but I have passed a day without money, and my memory serves me right, because I know it, Parent.

And where do you get money from, on the following day, child?

Well ⋯ I ⋯ hum ⋯ I ask for it from my family, friends or relatives—to help with what little they have. Or I just do something errand or odd for someone, and it is reciprocated as money. Splash, in your face! What do you have to say to that now, parent?

Well, why did or do you not ask for it the same day you do not have, or do something odd on that very day that will reciprocate money? This simply means that you made a choice of not having it that present day, in that moment. Because you know you already have it, in the next moment of the next day, no matter what, only when you ask or do something for it (so you rather hang on).

I tell you this: you have gone to bed with a dime, on that, and yet you still declared that you do not have money, thus disregarding what you have, and then pray, to have more of what you have lying beside you, again, instead of being thankful to multiply it. You are confusing your prayer. You are not sure of what you want and how much of it you want—and you keep on changing you mind about this. Because you are not sure that you have money, thus therefore it is very uncertain in your life, whether you have money or not. Instead of saying thank you, you complain and whine for some more. Thus that the process starts over again and again repetitively as you wake up to ask for it again. You think again, and it slowly comes as you go to it again, from a different newly reconstructed and re-made thought due to situation and condition, even if it is just right in your pocket or wallet, and or bank, child. And to what value is enough?!

Oh yah, value of worth right, Parent?
My friend, you have got it. You do remember.

Oh yah ⋯ now you are talking about forgetting to remember knowing, right, Parent?

You know it.

Oh ⋯ yes, yes ⋯ here, I got another one. Death of fear! Wow ⋯ I could just go on here and get a distinction, Parent.

And why is that child?
Because I know it!

Bravo, well-done. You are getting it! Ladies and gentlemen ⋯ I present to you —wait for it, wait for it. The greatest, the one and only ⋯ hum ⋯ what is your name again?

Really, Parent? Anyways, let us get back to it.
Good!

Now my good treasure of a child, this is what I say to you. Choose to take good care of what you pray for, because whatever you pray for the most, from your desire, will happen. Since that you now know that thought is a session of prayer in the moment expressing your choice of desire, therefore you should be aware of what you pray for in wanting, and this is to simply say that, be aware of what you think because you are creating it as a prayer in the moment of now. Now, know this. Whenever you think for something bad to happen to someone, you are thus therefore praying for it to happen. Because of thinking a lot about a bad thing that someone or somebody did to you; you then create thoughts that make you feel angry and furiously upset in your heart, thus in return as you deeply desire, you think and wish for bad things to happen to that person. I tell you this, it is within your heart of feelings that you create. Because your feelings from your heart create your reality, and this is to say that what you feel from your heart creates experiences of reality from thought, you have thus made a reality from desire on to things and on to people.

I tell you this, oh lovely great one. A church as group has cursed people and things by placing a word curse on them, in agony of dissatisfaction of their doings and, desire of vengeance from its thoughts. A church alone, singularly, privately in a room, has also done the same. I tell you this, oh great lovely one. A church as a group has blessed people and things by placing a word blessing on them, in jubilation of satisfaction and desire of goodness for their lives, from its thought. A church alone singularly, privately in a room, has also done this the same.

And now I tell you this oh great one, as a church that you are: You should choose to make your world a better place, by having good thoughts that give experiences of feeling from your heart, in this moment of prayer. The good things that you desire for and to yourself, desire them for your world as well, for you are in it. See to what it is that you hold as truth, for you are creating it as you believe by desire. Will you continue killing or cursing people or things by thoughts that you have about or on them? Or will you continue to let life live and bless people and things by thoughts that you have on them? Again, as any other moment, you have a choice from your thoughts as you create, to decide on how the world will turn out to be (your world). Now choose, in this moment, oh great church.

Wow, so all churches do that, Parent? A church prays for such things ⋯ And which church are you talking about exactly, because I know a lot?

Yes a church does this, and there is only one church in your world found in the universe. Only one in particular and no other, and it is everywhere and anywhere.

Okay, and what church is it, tell me, I want to know it Parent, so that I will never ever go and attend at that church at all or again anymore.

I tell you this, oh great child, there is only one church, and that church is you.

Me!

Yes, you child. Remember that everything that you do, and this is to say your breath, step and each and every action you make, you first think it. And what you think is your prayer in the moment for what you desire to be experienced, as you breathe and take a step towards it. You are the great grandest church because you pray every day. In one moment you are at a particular place or point experiencing your prayer in thought as it is manifested by being lived, and in the next, you are at another and, in the next after that, you are at another with others ⋯ so on ⋯ and on. You are moving to everywhere you think, to anywhere you know, seeking your desire as you think in prayer (spontaneously in action of movement).

Oh my good one, your body of flesh is a temple that is hosted by your great breath of soul. You are the holy one. You are the one that sings the hymns and psalms of what you believe in, from the way you think in your dream from cores of your heart. You are the one that is blessed and that blesses others. Every moment of time is holy blessed by your presence. Without you —the great holy one, holiness cannot be experienced. You are the church that I am talking about, and not any other, because there is not.

Now a church (meaning you), goes into a particular building, environment or place, of any name, at any time, because it wishes to experience itself collectively in what it believes in. When a church is in a group of same belief —its holiness increases and—desires are drawn more closely in attraction, due intensity and to the multiple number praying to and, for the same thing. This is the reason why a collective group of any sort, gets to achieve more of what they believe in, quicker. It happens because they have the same set of goals, and they help each other to achieve them, by thought of praying that attracts more and stronger of relevance, by doing and or a say of word. The greater the church, the greater the experience becomes because of a great number of multiple churches in one environment or building. And this meaning that, a lot of people in a building.

Now I tell you this. A building may crumble, a place may change and an environment may perish, and it will make no difference in your life. This is so, because you are the one that brings divine holy presence to any situation and place as a church you are already, at any moment. Now here is what happens: Whenever and wherever you are, and you pray, and believe from feeling that in that moment of prayer you are experiencing holiness, and you decide (just as you believe and have done), to make that place where you are praying at, a signified holy place, it will be just as so as you believe ⋯ You should read that sentence again child, for it holds your truth.

Mm, I saw and read that, Parent. I did.

Now, this simply means that, whatever place of any moment that you consider to only be experiencing holiness, it will be so as your truth of believe. When you only believe that you achieve and receive great holiness at a particular building and or from a special particular person at some moment, it will be so. Now with this great truth, it means that you consciously decide and discard any other place and or moment as not being holy, except the one that you only say is holy— and, you can change your mind about it. Again with this great phenomenal truth, you then miss the opportunity of experiencing and being holy every time, all the time, anywhere, everywhere, because you only say and believe that you receive holiness and great blessings at a particular place of believe or from a special person at particular time on a special day at some moment. Any place of environment or building does not carry or express emotion. You are the one with your greatness that brings life to any moment, anywhere. You are indeed the grand church.

Mm ⋯ wow I hear you. That is beautiful to know. Thank you for making me realize my self-worth and holiness with such sheer magnitude. I am grateful, Parent.

You welcomed, beautiful rose of universe.

Oh my good one, sing your song of great holy. Sing now in cheer for you are experiencing the holy moment, now. Look up and lift your hands now, in reach, and receive a blessing, now, for that is where the beautiful rays of the sun, the gentle soft rain, and twinkling stars fall from to bless the land that you stand on, on your feet, and say thank you, I receive. Oh my good one, look down and lower your hands now, in reach, and take a blessing, for that is where the beautiful blessings that you have received have fallen on, and are growing to satisfy you, and say thank you, I am pleased.

Oh great one that is entrusted with all, enjoy and celebrate. Be great for all experiences for you have felt and lived them as wished as you are now. Let your heart pump completeness and let your mind receive it, for you do not lack. You have everything in the universe. Boom and blossom from the fertile taste of the earth, and cleanse yourself with pure morning dew that refreshes and quenches the thirst of beauty of desire. Be nourished and stretched to the everlasting seed of your plough. Today of this moment is yours to be great and filled with happiness of life. Right now, at this moment, it is your time to shine brighter than you are.

Wow that is beautiful—such sweet words. Was that a prayer for me or were you blessing me, Parent?

Once more again my treasure of a child, I am making you realize of who you truly potently are beyond your current imagination of creation. You are more than what you are, and will always be.

Well, what can I say? Thank you once more again, oh good Parent of love.
You are welcomed, all the time of universe, child.

Now listen again for this is the meaning of prayer and the power to produce, and it is happening now in this moment because it is yours. A prayer is a great force that does not force. This meaning that a prayer is a force itself that lets go of the pulling and pushing of desire. It is comfortable acceptance that surrenders and acknowledges that all that is desired is available and in possession. This simply means that where there is force and tension in attraction between any joint links of wanting and not wanting—with prayer, all pressure is released and let loose. This happens because it is within a deep engaged moment of prayer that a reality of love is lived to be experienced accordingly. This is to say that things are let to fulfill their purpose by their own highest choice rather than being precluded and pulled, dragged or pushed, which in turn creates a back and forth movement at a fixed single point or, create unpleasant snapped scattered results of desire in displacement.

This is why when you, child, pray, feel powerless and overtaken by liberty and rapture of various emotions of not being in charge of the situation, yet rather allowing it to take course to cause, because you learn and remember to accept and leave things to your higher self and live this now moment as you experience your wants and request as they come to you already in their existence, when you pray. This is so because prayer is an affirmed and confirmed reality of want and desire from thought of choice process.

Now, here is the power of prayer: For you to be able to experience your wants and wishes, you have to choose to realize, just as we said before that, all is available and you are already in possession of it just by thinking of it. When you hold this truth with you; you will then be able to mostly do the things you love because you know that what you wish and want, you own or it is coming to you already. With this truth thereof, should you find yourself in a moment or situation that you will define as difficult and or bad, or not knowing what to do, you should choose to say thank you to what is coming to make it better. When this is done, you then let your wishes take course.

Wow, mm ··· hallelujah—Amen!

There you go, and that it is all you have to say. Just say, ("*kea leboha*", "*asante*", "*shakuran lak*" and "*si si nie*").

Well then it goes without saying, Parent.
Indeed it does··· child.

Oh child of universe of creation. The one painted with sparkles and glitter of everlasting life from the colors of rainbow that pierce through the spectrum of rain dew in the sky to marvelously reveal beauty. The one that is forever granted wishes and desire. Present your breath of soul to yourself in this moment for prayer. Be here complete, for you are to have divine truth of prayer to gain what you will want and wish to have.

Now this is what I tell you: The main obstacle between you and for your prayer is doubt and worry. Most often frequent of time after you have prayed, you then place a thought of (what if) what you have prayed for does not happen, which in turn creates deflated feelings of sad emotions of what might not. This meaning that you move your attention away from what will be, and what you prayed for, for else other that is not, which is what you did not pray for (initially).

This shifting of thought and re-inventing feelings, thus then creates doubt and worry concerning your condition and current situation. Doubt and worry which was never there before to begin with. When doubt has immersed and clouded itself into your thoughts and has oppressed your heart, you do not see the thing that you prayed for, coming to you, which then causes you to disbelieve in its existence and coming. Then after having less faith in disbelieve, when looking at your situation or target, you then become frustrated by it because you see the same condition and state, and not of that you prayed for. All these emotions when put together, they then create worry. Therefor worry is a sibling or a child of doubt that you yourself create by choosing to not know that you will always have, and that it is coming. When worried, situations are aggravated through the intensified and dense thoughts about how they are, which then never creates solutions but rather the same harshened and hardened results of what has always been, in your experience of now. It is doubt and worry that puts a barrier and confines you in a room of fear. Fear then stops you ultimately from doing at all.

Now listen beautiful child, for this is what I say: For you to be able not to experience stress through doubt and worry, you have to understand only to realize that you are in a predicament that can be exited. This is to simply say and mean that, when in an unpleasant and unfavorable situation, you should know that you are there in it already, now, in that moment of experience, and that your gift of prayer is coming just as you thought to choose it, and not your current state anymore. Again, this is to emphasize that you should only concentrate on the things that you want by thinking about them through prayer because they do not worry or stress you, yet rather motivates and encourages—and, you do not have doubt when you think, imagine or see them, yet in obverse, you do get tensed, stressed, worried and full of doubt when you think about what you do not want. It is only through knowing that, all fear, worry and doubt will disappear when you have prayed, because you know that all exists and that only desired realities are experienced when only ultimately chosen by being concentrated on, rather than what is not. (just ignore to forget what is not).

Mm ⋯ yeah ⋯ wow. I hear you, Parent. I just had to keep quiet and listen. Well you did good then, my one and only.

Now listen, for this is how you have determined your situations and gifts of desire in your dream by levels within a prayer. Within moments of desired creation and desperate frustrated realities, you place fulfillment of an outcome to certain degree to be achieved or acquired. That is to say that, most often, you hope for an outcome of a certain type in particular; then after, you create faith from hope for that outcome; after that, you then create believe for and on what you pray for. In obvious general sense, this means that, you hope, have faith and then believe. These are your levels at which you measure the success of acquiring something and getting a particular result from a prayer.

With that having been said, this also determines where you are in position according to these levels, to realize or materialize what you want in your dream. This is to ultimately say that, when you have hope, you will be hoping and nothing other than that, on that level. And when you have faith, you acknowledge that it is there and or coming, at that level. And when you believe, it is when you now know that it has always been there and all that you had or have to do, to begin with, was to believe, at that level. And now I tell you this, my fair good child. Since each level positions you, you should choose the ultimate one.

Okay, meaning what Parent?

Meaning that everything exists, including what you want in all-that-is. Therefor for much greater emphasis on what I have mentioned before, this means that, instead of hoping you should know that it is there. Instead of having faith, you should know that it will be as it is. Instead of believing, you should know that it is. For when you hope, you are questioning the very existence and reality of it, which creates doubt and worry. Why should you hope on what is? For when you have faith, you are questioning the very existence and reality of it, which creates doubt and worry. Why should you have faith on what is? For when you believe, you are questioning the nature of its existence and reality, which creates doubt and worry. Why should you believe when it is already like that? All you have—is to know that it is, and that you have, and it will.

Mm ⋯ okay, I hear fair Parent. So now tell me, are you saying that I should not hope, have faith nor believe?

Oops, you missed me there. You must have been distracted by a little extra more reading. No child, I am saying and making you realize the levels of consciousness of creating in your dream, to have what you want from prayer. For only when you truly know that what you want, already exists, you will not have hope, seek to have faith and nor believe (or even pray), for it is there, and all that you have to do is to thank its availability, creation and existence, and just take. Once you are at a full conscious level that you have already, you will not use any of the above mentioned levels to have what you want, now in your dream.

Wow ⋯ mm it makes sense now. Thank you, Parent. And I have another question here for you. Is there any type or form of formal or informal for that matter, of prayer I should follow or say every time, or is that it?

Yes there is, child.
Okay, and what is it, Parent?

Any!
Any prayer, Parent?

Yes, any!

Oh wow ⋯ great. Annie are you okay, are you okay Annie. Annie are you okay, are you okay ⋯ Annie! Yay hooray ⋯ Michael Jackson is in the building y' all.

Hah, hah, hah ⋯ there you go! Any is okay indeed, my good child.
Okay, so we are done with prayer?

Well that is if you do not want anything else in or from life, then yes we done, child.

Oh come on, you know what I mean.
Yes we are my lovely one.

SEXUAL WAR

This is what love says

Oh my sweet child, my great beautiful child. You are sexy and hot, there is no any other more beautiful than what you are. Your body stands out because it was made and is of the awesome majestic beautiful orchid that creates and pumps the universe. I admire everything about your body just the way it is. It is pleasing and desirable. I see all that is good because you were never made of anything that is not. Your beauty is painful and in the process, it literally breaks your heart because you have to prove that it is really beautiful and that it exists. You my lovely have done it, yes you are ingeniously greatly beautiful, child.

Now I say this unto you. You have to agree to this, for when you choose not to, you are choosing to will it not to be agreed on, and it is all okay in goodness of your choice. And this is what I say—

Agree to this:

Whenever you are born and you die on birth—you give life to death through birth. And also just as it is, whenever you are born and you live on birth, you give birth to life.

And also just as it is, to the one that creates and gives birth, whenever you die —through giving birth; you give birth to death as so you may have a different living, being it that which you have given life to. And also just as it is, to the one that create and gives birth, whenever you live—through giving birth, you give birth to life as so you may have a different living, being it that which you have given life to (and become the witness of yourself and testify your past for a new course in correction).

Wow okay ⋯ wow really, I am running out of words of what to say. I am really breath-full. So what are you trying to say though, Parent?

I am not trying anything, I am only saying this: Whenever you die, someone will live for you only just for love. And whenever you live, someone will die for you only just for love.

Yeah I hear you, but why?
Because you ask for it!

What?
Love!

Okay! So now tell me Parent. What sexual war are you talking about?

I am talking about the sexual war that you have engaged in with yourself as a whole being, to determine your sexuality, child. You are fighting yourself because of sex, and you do not see it. Instead of accepting yourself as you are already as a being of both sex, you have willed to be a man rather than a woman. You also have willed to be a woman rather than a man. At this moment you have clearly chosen to be a man by willing to have all the characteristics and feature that symbolizes and represent him, as you have identified it. You also, at this very moment, have clearly chosen to be a woman by willing to have all the characteristics and feature that symbolizes and represent her, as you have identified it. In all of this controversy about who you clearly are in representation, you still will not to see that you are a woman and a man—: Did you hear that child?

I am a bit confused Parent, what are you talking about exactly? What are you getting to?

I am saying this child. As long as you claim and reveal that you are a man by genital symbolism, and that the other is a woman, then you are saying that a woman is not a man. And also as long as you claim and reveal that you are a woman by genital symbolism, and that the other is a man, then you are saying that a man is not a woman.

Well ⋯ hum, is it not the way it is supposed to be? I mean isn't it the way it is Parent?

Yes as you say it, child. And this is what I will tell now: You are a man and you are a woman. You are a being of both, in one body. You will now ever be together in peace and not separated. The two beings of opposite sex are just right inside of you and on you in existence. This is exactly what you are in war with, yet you struggle to see it.

You are in a great war with yourself, and nothing other. You will to fail to clearly see, even though it is just right inside of you and on you, you still do not see that both beings are what is and has created you. You start off with a simple thought in suggestion of all great possible things in the world that can be done and experienced only by choice. Which then; (this choice of yours) from what you think, creates a talk of conversation, that turns out to be an argument of doubt in disagreement of what you want and should choose holistically, which then also, wills you to harm your own body by fighting it towards feeling it—as pain.

Wow ⋯ what? I missed that one, Parent. You might just have to elaborate on that. What did you say?

Listen child, be present in soul for this concerns your sexuality, and this what I am saying: When you will not to lay a hand on a woman, you should choose to will not to lay a hand on a man because they are fairly equally both inside and on you. I tell you this, as long as a woman is hurt, then you have hurt that woman. As long as a man is hurt, then you have hurt that man.

A woman or a man is hurt when the other opposite sex of the same being disagrees with. Every time when you say "No!" to that woman inside of you and on you, as a man, by repudiating, just know that you have hurt that woman because you will have rejected her as she is and of what she thinks as a woman. Also know that every time when you say "No!" to that man inside of you and on you as a woman by repudiating, just know that you have hurt that man because you will have rejected him as he is and of what he thinks as a man.

Okay ⋯ then what should I choose to do Parent?

Well I recommend that you choose to make peace with a woman and love her ⋯ have love with her. And also choose to make peace with a man and love him ⋯ have love with him. Choose both sides, because it is who you are holistically in the anatomy of a being, and you cannot be without. Have them agree to their fair own equal best interest.

Wait ⋯ on that very same subject, are you saying that I should also love and sleep with the same type of sex?

This is exactly how you think child, and you have just missed what I have just told you. If you keep this form of thinking, then the war inside of you and on you will not stop because you will be creating the same difference against the other opposite sex that is in and on your body. By this I mean, you will believe that same is attractive, and that the other that is different in opposite, is not attractive, which in this case is either woman or a man.

90

So should I choose to sleep with both different sexes, Parent?

I tell you this, sleep only with yourself as a man and as a woman as you already are (and this is what you failing yourself to see). By this I mean that you should acknowledge that there is a great feminine side part of you as you are—genetically, in and on you. You should also acknowledge that there is a great masculine side part of you as you are—in and on you. You do not have to sleep with any either of them because they are already inside of you, having sex to create you as a whole being, right now in this moment.

Mm ⋯ I still do not quite understand, Parent.
Well; worry yourself not, for I am explaining this mystery and phenomena to you now.

Now I say this to you child. It is within this confusion, it is within this uncertainty about yourself as a being that is a man-woman, that you do not know yourself. Because of the very reason that you are so not sure, and are unclear that both beings are present in you and on you; you thus struggle to make decisions. You do this because you do not trust the feminine side part or the masculine side part—that is of you, because you think and do not see the other as you, and that they are inside of you, hence you are never so sure on what to decide on. You have confused yourself, struggled, fought and argued with yourself for a long time thus it is as such that all the confusion, struggles, fights and arguments you have had within yourself are projected outwards from within you, to the world for a long time. Now, because of all of this, (your projections of who you are from the above mentions) have created your surrounding in and on this world. Only just right now, because of failing to accept and realize yourself as a singular being that is a polarity of two sexes moving on equilibrium within yourself, you still have war.

Wait a minute ⋯ let us rewind and step back a few paces here Parent. Are you saying that all the wars that have taken place are not caused by race, color, power, territorial land and or over resources?

Yes they are. They are because you have listened to a man or women—to have one side of you satisfied over the other, child. Instead of agreeing with yourself, together as both holistically for one common goal, you have chosen one over the other—of yourself, as being.

How so Parent?

Hush ⋯ let me break down for you. This is what you have observed from a man inside of you and on you, and have thus identified him as such:

- A man is about strength.
- A man is about power.
- A man is about force.
- A man is about defending and fighting.
- A man is about braveness and fearlessness.
- A man is about protection and preservation.
- A man is about anger.
- A man is about love.

And now, this is what you have observed from a woman inside of you and on you, and have thus identified her as such:

- A woman is about jealousy
- A woman is about envy.
- A woman is about hate.
- A woman is about happiness.
- A woman is about kindness and gentleness.
- A woman is about giving.

- A woman is about desire and pleasure.
- A woman is about love.

You see child, the two side parts are different and yet not separated. There is only you deciding and, feeling the way you choose, and then label what form or part of you should experience and express that feeling right from inside of you (meaning either a man or woman). Now be present with and in soul, be currently here now, for what I am about to say requires a lot of focus and attentive concentration.

Listen, a woman and a man's emotional characteristics reciprocate interchangeably like a pendulum, in one being. By this I mean that characteristics are transferred and drawn back to and fro on each side part of a being. A being as you are, is of only creation, and creation is of only a polarity that repels itself to a different flow of movement and form to create itself as duality and or even multiples.

Hum ⋯ I kind of get you, but not entirely. What do you mean by that, Parent?

Okay listen, just be bearing with me on this one. This is what I am saying: Should you happen to experience feeling jealous, envious and or hate, you should recognize and be aware that, that feeling characterizes a woman side part of you that you are. With that said, it moves forth and back. This means that it swings to the man's side part of you and back where it came, which is the woman's side part of you—or in obverse. Now like I said before, should you happen to experience feeling jealous, envious and or hate towards someone or something, and you recognize or be aware of it, you should next observe and be aware of how you act or portray that feeling. See what or which emotional characteristic will you use to express or overcome that feeling.

Will you fight as a man that you already are, to show how jealous and envious you are as woman, to claim what you are jealous towards, or of? Will you use force, strength, might and or power to show how better you can do it, as a man, just to show how jealous, envious and hateful you are feeling as a woman that you already are? Which emotional characteristic will you choose, child? And that is all that you have or should choose to do, just decide, uniformly. The ultimate decision is of both, and not any of either of the being inside of you as you.

Wow, now that is some insight Parent. So what you are saying is that, if I feel jealous, envious or hateful towards someone or something because of what they have, I am acting as and portraying characteristics of a woman?

Yes child, indeed.

And if I force or fight against someone or something because of what they have, in jealousy, I am acting as and, portraying characteristics of a man because of what I feel as a woman. Also if I defend and protect, I am being a man to keep and have the things I desire and please me as woman.

Yes! Yes that is how it is, you nailed it! You just took it home with you ⋯ you took it all the way with you. Now you are getting closer to great understanding, child. I am so happy when you understand. And this is what pleases me. Wow ⋯ and it is so good to see you smiling. Look at you all smileys and full it.

Ah ⋯ just stop it, you making me blush here and, a bit shy. I am having goosebumps and it feels a bit awkward, Parent.

Well I guess that must be the woman side of you, feeling that way, and I must be doing something stimulatingly good to her. I wonder what it is.

Hah, hah, hah ⋯ Oh my word, there we go again, Parent. And this is the time when I say, 'okay ⋯ can we calm down a bit, otherwise we might just get carried away and lose focus on important subjective objectives.'

Yes, I will have to agree with you as a whole on that, child.
You mean you will not choose a woman or a man over the other, but agree with both?

My good friend you know me.
Yes, I think I am getting to, Parent.

Now listen, my fair good child. Be here with me, for I am revealing what has been complicated and confusing. This is very confusing for you, as it has, thus you still do not know who you are. And I am here, to expose you, to yourself in the open as so you may be assured and know who you are. So bear with and be very attentive.

Now listen to this, when I said that the wars have occurred because you have listened to a woman or a man, right inside and on you. I meant exactly that, yet this does not mean that he or she is making a choice for you, because since you are the one who is listening, you get to make the choice as woman or a man, or wholly both as one (which would be of great best interest as a whole), and that is to say as you, even if what is said comes from you.

And that means what, Parent?

When a woman feels all hateful, jealous and envious of desire towards someone, and she suggests and tells you of it, and or you feel that you should attack and fight that someone for her, for what that other has, by taking it from them. Then it is to you, to see her as a woman feeling that way with emotional characteristics of a woman, and yet talking of, or saying, portraying and acting out emotional characteristics of a man as an expression from inside of her. And you, as a person who is listening, you get to choose and decide if whether you agree to attack and fight someone to take what they have, for a woman that desires what they have, that is characterizing a man.

And also know this again, that if you agree to attack and fight, you are using your man' s emotional characteristics to agree with that woman' s self-portrayed characteristics of a man, because you will feel the same way as that woman, yet act out as a man you are already (both). You would choose and make a choice to attack and fight for her, and that is to say her emotions of woman, as a man you are, and she will support you as a man she is – correlative in characterized emotions of a man, and remain behind as woman that she physically is, in appearance.

In other terms or words, what I have just said means that, whenever and whomever you listen to, whether a man or a woman. You should be attentive and careful of what you take from what is said, and how you choose to act from the voiced motives of a person. When you act on certain implied motive from a person, because of some feeling they have, which may represent any feature of either a man or woman, then it means that you have connected to an understanding of that featured representation on its level.

When you understand that particular feature from another person, you come to understand yourself as that which is portrayed and act like it, be it a man or woman, thus as such that you are talking and understanding yourself externally as you do internally opposite or the same. Therefore whenever you act on someone' s influence, see if you agree wholly together internally. This is to say wholly internally as a man and woman you are already inside of you.

And if you do, see if you also agree wholly together externally—this is to say wholly externally as physically characterized as you are, in appearance, together with the other person as physically characterized as they are as either a man or woman without any doubt. Now this means that if you choose to fight or go to war for either a man or woman (for any reason), go together in support and righteousness. If and when there is one behind, then there is disagreement to that fight or war, because you are not in it together, holistically, as a being, and it is clearly (externally seen, by physical appearance).

Hum ⋯ you getting to something here, but you are not articulating it well, dearest Parent.

Well it is just that you do not understand the polarity that you are, of which I am explaining right now, dearest child.

Very well then, this is what I am saying, to you, man child. When and if you do decide to fight or go to war, take your wife with you, and or also take your daughter with you; when she refuses, then that means she does not support that fight or war, even if she may have suggested and told you about it, from the powerful and defensive characteristic features of a man that she has (inside of her).

Now, I say this, to you, woman child. When and if you do decide to fight or go to war, take your husband with you, and or also take your son with you; when he refuses, then that means he does not support that fight or war, even if he may have suggested it from the hateful and jealous characteristic features of a woman that he has (inside of him).

This complex polarity can better be understood by introspectively hearing and knowing yourself. This is to say that, when you do, or choose and agree on a particular thing. See if you have any doubt and or are questioning the very act of it, and if any, also see which and what characteristics influence and represent that doubt or act, against or in support of the choice you are making. Is it of a man or woman? And when you cannot feel or hear anything from within you, therefor then, you should choose to observe it from outside

97

of you in reflection. This meaning that, see if your opposite sex agrees and responses positively to it, because it is an external representation of what you have and are feeling from inside of you already, yet it is mirrored so that you may know and see yourself, as you think. From the observation that you make of your opposite sex, you are then able to identify which characteristics of feelings are against your decision, and which one you are using.

Now, clearly, you have not, and still do not wholly agree to war thus as such that you mostly find a woman part of you choosing to stay at home, and is opposing. A woman most of the time, stays at home because she refuses to fight or go to war—because she is against it, (for her it is obscured)—especially physical. And remember that, that woman remaining behind, represents your internal characterized feelings in physical appearance. So then, this means that you go to war or fight, yet you do not feel okay, alright and just about it, even if you suggested it internally and externally from and as yourself.

Whoa ⋯ okay ⋯ okay, I got it. Wow, I really do see and understand what you mean. It took a while, but phew, I have it, up here ⋯ and in my heart, Parent.

Good! Very good, you are.

Now listen, child. Oh my good lovely child, as a man that you are ⋯ love that woman. Love that woman because she is all that you have, besides the man you are already. That woman has been there for you in all-ways, she has been your place of desire and comfort. When you could not tell any other your secret, you chose to tell and share with her your secret. Love that woman as you love, cherish and appreciate yourself, because she has taken care of you. She has bathed you, she has willed, by sacrificing her desires as so you may be fed, well raised and have a proper good education. That woman has struggled, argued and fought with you from birth, to turn you into the right man you are today, when no man could, yet you still argue with her in marriage. Even when you refused to listen to her, she afterwards held you close to her chest and gave you a kiss of comfort, and told you that everything will be okay, and that she loves you. That woman has willed to understand, accept and be with you through all your faults and selfish acts. I tell you this, man child, it was, and is a woman that took care of you and provided for you. She is the one, more than any other man, that has told you that she loves you, and indeed she does love you. You have kissed, seen and slept with that woman nude from young, and you still do see her nude and sleep with her in marriage because she trusts you, and wills you to feel where you come from by feeling her womb. It is where you came from you love the most; because you came from a good place, hence you love to feel and taste where you came from. Therefore be gentle as the slow cool ocean breeze on her, be sweet as honey to her, caress and tell that woman that you love her. Appreciate and glorify that woman.

Now listen, child. Oh my good lovely child, as a woman that you are ⋯ love that man because he has in all-ways been there for you when no any other woman could. He has and still is, going an extra mile, by working relentlessly hard and making sure that you have all that you need and desire. He has defended and fought for you physically, even when you did not ask him—to show and prove to you how much he loves you. That man raised you into a woman that you are today. It is that man you have shared and told your secrets to when no other woman could understand you. He has been the one who has stood strong as pillar of a mountain for you. He is the one that has raised your esteem, even though you did not feel worth, he held you proudly in public without any shame of you, and declared you as his. You have kissed, seen and slept with that man nude from young, and you still do see him nude and sleep with him in marriage because he trusts you. I tell you this, it is that man that makes you feel good inside about yourself, thus you do go back for more of what makes you feel good inside as woman. Therefore be kind, and respect that man for who he is. Be patient and humble yourself, caress and be gorgeously awesome for and to that man. Glorify and praise his nature by embracing it, and tell that man that you love him.

I do hear you good Parent. I am here in soul. So now tell me here, dearest. You have been mentioning and telling me that I consist of a polarity with two different forms of sex, and this is to say a man and woman. How are they about in me? I would like to understand this.

Ah ⋯ the answer to that is very simple, and you know that answer. But very well then, I will remind you, here, once more again, child.

Now, you were taught, and you have learned that, for you to exist in this form, you are created by a man and a woman—(for obvious reasons). You know that a woman and a man both have 48 chromosomes and, that they are split in half from each respective individual to later meet by merging through a penetration connection of intercourse by both beings, as so they may be the wholly 48, again, as they were. You know that it is these chromosomes that, carries each characteristic of a woman and a man to form you. They are embedded within you, as you. And apart from what you were taught in school and told by your parents—you have observed and seen how a being is formed. You have personally engaged in such creative activities of forming and creating a being.

Yah I know that, Parent ⋯ I was kind of looking for a more abstract and profound rationality. Something that could wow me ⋯ you know, like you have done before.

I know that, child. You always have these questions in your head and, you always search for meaning and patterns to your questions. You love to wonder and figure out what is really going on here. I mean what is going on here, especially with you, in your dream.

Yah ⋯ nah ⋯ You got me. That is me, for sure, right there.

Don't you worry child, I have some more of that good profound stuff that you like so much. So brace yourself, because I am coming hard again, and this time there is no holding back, I am going all the way, but I will be easy on you.

Gosh, what! Oh my word, what did you just say ⋯? You know what? Just forget about it.

Okay good, now are you ready, child?
What am I even supposed to say? Should I even say yes to that, Parent?

I am serious here, child.
Okay ⋯ okay, I am with you. So let's do it, now, let us begin.

Now be present, with your flesh and bones. Be here wholly both, together with spirit, mind, soul and heart desire, for I am sharing and telling you the grandest truth of your time in the universe. This is your love for dreams, and you love making dreams. Everything is created within a dream, therefore this is the truth of creative love and about love of dreams. I am telling you, now, right here, why there is male and female, and how they are inside of you.

Wow ⋯ now that sounds very profound, Parent. I am ready, now ⋯ actually I am more than ever ready. I am ready to take it all in, and you got me all excited and steamed up.

Good, now here it comes, child. Female and male are creators and creation themselves, in a dream—

Aha ⋯ don't stop, please carry on.

Stop being silly and playful, and pay attention, child. I am serious here.
Okay ⋯ I will let you do your thing, I won't interrupt you, I promise.

Now listen, and be here, child. Without female and or male, there is no experience of creation. Therefore for definite reasons, ultimately and absolutely surely as guaranteed, sex is for creation. For creation to be about, that is to say to experience its existence, you as a singular being, in a dream, split yourself as so to realize yourself. When you remain singular in a dream, there is no creation, in experience of it because there is only you in that dream of yours. You cannot be yourself when you already are yourself in a dream. The more of your same self you create, the more of your same self you become. This means that you experience yourself as the same, and thus therefore create nothing but yourself as you are already, in your dream of what you choose to be and, where to be it. For example: if the same sets or pair of twins (the same in gender) keep on reproducing themselves the same in multiples of dozens, then that means there is only one person all over the same everywhere, and therefore does not know itself different, because it is the same!

Okay parent, I just have to stop you there. I mean this is confusing now, it sounds as if you are repeating and reiterating and saying the same thing over and over again in different ways. And are we talking about dreams already?

Yes, child, I know. Well that is how sex is. It is very confusing hence you never know how to explain the feeling ⋯ no matter how many different ways you try. Now, I am explaining the same thing in different ways, because if I say it only in one way, you are as assured definitely to ask what do I mean by that, and I will have to explain, still, in another different way. And that is why I have to change style even if it is the same principle. And yes we have been talking about dreams. The first word that you read when you held this in your arms, was and still is dreams, but as of this point we are not in depth within that subject.

Okay ⋯ I hear you, Parent. That is actually true.

Now listen. There is only one being in a dream, and you as a being, create all that you experience and all that you see, in it. A being has all emotions of feeling, and has no particular form, especially considering sexual gender. Now, since a being is not in any form, particularly, and has and, consist of all emotions of feeling, it only experiences itself, nothing else but it, only and wholly, emotionally. Therefore with this truth, all the emotions of feeling that there are—are mixed up all together without differentiating themselves as they are, as so to feel and be as one just as the creator, and or creation is one itself.

Okay ⋯ and what is this feeling of all emotions mixed up together, Parent?

Love! Like I said before, child, love is dreams and dreams are love, and you love making dreams and to create. And all that is created comes from you, in your dream—from love!

Okay ⋯ I am still with you, Parent.

Good. Now listen very closely, for it is about to get bumpier and rougher rugged.

Okay good, again, I am still with you, Parent.

Now listen, for this is your truth, and this is what a being did, and does. With all the emotions mixed up altogether, a being decided and, decides to split, and classify all the emotions that are one into two categories. It does this as so to see itself different, because when it is only one, (and being it so it is formless)—it does not see itself but only feels itself, thus as such that it only knows what it is feeling. And when a being forms itself into any particular form of kind that is one and singular, it will not see that form it is, because it will not be looking or observing it, thus it will end up not knowing what it created of itself, and so it is thus as such that it will have created itself into what it does not know, and therefore becomes formless because it does not know what shape or form it is, but only feels it as itself.

Okay ⋯ now I do understand your repetition I really do hear, and understand what you are saying, Parent.

Good. We can move on.

Now, with all the emotions of feeling split apart from one being; a being created itself into a form, from one particular group of classified emotions of feeling. This means that each group of emotions of feeling (of the two), formed themselves into separate beings. The other being holds certain information of the whole being, and the other also holds certain information of the same whole being. With the duality of the same having being established, it was, and still is able to see the other form that it is, from a different perspective of itself, that it did not know and understand before—but could feel.

Now, the two forms of beings, classified and categorized uniquely characteristically, they form themselves into beings that are able to discharge information that holds their characteristics, that then merge together to form and recreate the same first being with all the mixed emotions of feelings as either one of them. Therefore this means that, the halves of the whole being, that were split, come together again, to form the first creator. And that creator that is re-created, having both characteristics mixed again, as one, can and will choose to express them as either one of any of the two self-created forms of the one being that were split from itself (meaning either male or female, or whatever it thinks and sees itself to be, as it imagines).

Mm ⋯ I do understand now, Parent. Wow ⋯ then that means you have been right all this time. I mean yes, you are right, when you say that I am one being with two polarities. I am both man and woman, or should I say man-woman. Oh wow, oh my word and, that is why some people would say that I look like my mother, and some would say I look like my father.

Well yes, child ⋯ for obvious reasons.

Yes, yes, I know Parent. But even if I look like both my parents, yet at the same time I look like me, and they do not look like me, because I can tell the difference because of my uniqueness. Wow ⋯ and I have to admit again, and say that, 'yes, you are right' when you say that, "Therefore for definite reasons, ultimately and absolutely surely as guaranteed, sex is for creation." I mean this is all starting to make sense now, and the answers were obviously there all the time! I am a man-woman!

Yes, child you are, and they are both in you and on you. For you to understand a woman, it means that you put yourself in her position, and the only way you do this, is when you use your feminine characterized emotions of feeling as a woman. And when you do this, you thus understand that woman because you become her by (literally) being in her place. Also, for you to understand a man, it means that you put yourself in his position, and the only way you do this, is when you use your masculine characterized emotions of feeling as a man. And when you do this, you thus understand that man because you become him by being in his place. This is the reason why you would find that, what you do sometimes represents either a man or woman, even though you are physically presenting yourself as what you are now (in appearance)!

Everything that you do, represents exactly that. The way you walk, bend, cross or spread legs, dance, dress and sleep, and have sex, is the same way as you would wholly as either a man or woman. Your concerns about self-image, beauty and make up, your formality and informality, represents who you are as whole, and you reveal them as you physically are, already from any characterized emotions of feeling.

Okay, Parent. Straight up, I hear you. Wow ⋯ sex is for creation, and I am a man-woman!

Yes, child. Now there is more to this, than the way you have understood from my explanation. Sex is broadened and ambiguous creation, and I am here to explain it. So don't you worry, I have more of that profound good stuff that you like so much ⋯ I am going to give it to you until you beg me to stop.

Whoa ⋯ that sounds too much, but I like it though. So yah, you can give it to me all you want and like, I will take it all in. I will handle it! I can take it.

Good, very good, child. Here it comes.

Now I tell you this, again child. Sex is for creation. Whatever you can put your mind to, everything that you see and think of, is created through sex for experience.

Everything! Created ⋯ through sex? Hum ⋯ I am not sure about that, Parent.

Yes, child. Everything is created through sex—(for the experience of its choice), and whatever it is that is created, has to mix its particles with its same type, to create the same type, and or mix with a different type, to create a different type.

Okay ⋯ and that is supposed to mean what, Parent? I still do not understand how everything is made from sex. I mean I do understand how a man and a woman are created, and that they are in me, but as for everything else being

106

created through sex ⋯ that just does not get through to me. I mean how is this all possible?

Well, believe it or not, child, the answer is so simple that, you will think small of yourself for not knowing and thinking to this extend.

Okay, and what is it, Parent?

Now listen, here is the truth in plain sight. This is a revelation, that the duality of one creates everything. For water to be, it requires hydrogen and oxygen. Each individual separate atom come together and, emits and merges to connect and create water. Water is the wholly substance of hydrogen and oxygen. Without either, it does not exist as it is. For water to be more of itself, it has to mix with itself as water. And for water to create something more other than itself, it has to mix with that which is different from itself. And whatever it is that is created from water, and that which is different, has to mix with more of its same type, to create more of itself the same, and or mix with a different type, to create another different type—it is a continuing ripple cycle.

This process continues and accounts for everything. Creation itself is a symmetrical orgy of particles of one being. Atoms form molecules of the same or different, and molecules form compounds of the same or different, and compounds form substances of the same or different, and also substance form material of the same or different. All particles come together in pairs, of the same or different, to merge, mix and make love and exchange information to create anew as desired—ideally. It is an ever ongoing process until nothing is desired to be created, by a being, such as you are.

Wow ⋯ okay. That is mind blowing ⋯ I don't know what to say, Parent. So you really mean that everything is created by two things, forms, object, particles or beings, of the one?

Yes, it is so, child. Everything that you see now, in this present moment of yours, is created through two particles of the one, that come together and, have sex by merging their individual characteristics to create a desired particular thing, that may be the same or different.

Now listen, again, for I am telling and sharing to you more of your divine truth. You have these two beings that are characteristically categorized in within you already. Now, with these two beings inside of you, it means that you can, and will create anything and everything that you wish and desire, from them, singularly wholly holistically.

Wait ⋯ what! Anything and, everything! You see, this is exactly what you do. You get me all excited and ecstatic about things, and you know I do not understand how things are done. Which in the end, I have to ask, how can all of this be done, Parent?

Well at least I am not getting you all worked up for nothing, and leaving you clueless. I tell you this, child; I am here, now, all the time with you. You do not even have to worry about anything, because I have dedicated myself to helping you, yet only by your choice and will, if so you will let me.

Thank you, I appreciate it. Now tell me, how can I, and will I create anything?

Good, very good. Because you are quite avid, you shall as you have willed, have your answer, child.

Be centered, child, for I am telling you how to create. This is the truth of your now dream. Having both beings, opposite in character and sex, already inside of you, it means that you can create anything and everything. You are one whole being, consisting of two polarities of the same. Therefore first, before all creation of experience, this means that, you as one whole complete being, can and may create another being without having to have sex physically as you now formally know and understand traditionally. This significant and marvelously wonderful divine truth is possible, as it is already happening, because the two beings are genetically mating right now, and this is to say having sex, and exchanging information inside of you, while creating and birthing you anew (through your ideas).

Okay, Parent. Hum ⋯ I seem to be catching two things here. First, I can create a being without having sex, and secondly, in the process I am also being created, is that right?

Yes, it is, child. You are being created by yourself. Now, like I said before, there is more to sex than what you just simply understand. Therefore, be patient and see to clearly understand.

Okay, I see, Parent.

Good. Now, for you to change, and have new and fresh features, is because two opposite genetic cells come together and, have sex to create new ones for the whole, (and that is to say you as a whole). Without any new born cells (replicated), your state would and will not change. And any now new different feature, that you did not have before, it arose because two different cells of the whole, come together to create a different new one, or thing, because it is required by the whole to present what it thinks of itself from within.

So you are saying that, everything that I have, even inside just as outside on me, I have it because I required it, Parent?

Well not necessarily require, yet rather show, because producing it means you always had it just as you have now ⋯ and yes, as a whole, you did. Some time ago you had no beard and, pubic hair around your genitals, but now you do because you required it to resemble yourself as a man. Sometime ago you had no breasts and such curves and hair on your genital, but now you do because you required it to resemble yourself as a woman, child.

Wow ··· then that means I am mix of internal cross breed of cells creating whatever it is I require as whole. This means that you are right, when you say that there is more to sex than what I now know and understand.

Yes there is my good friendly child?
Wow, okay ··· I am still listening to you, Parent.

Good, very good you are.

Now, again child, mellow and clear your ears. Present your whole state of being, and be in the moment, for I am reminding you of your forgotten truth. This is the grandest truth of creation. Your dreams are created through sex thoughtfully imaginatively to have your desires met. Now, to create a being internally, you have to choose to come to full clarity and understanding of who you are as a whole holistically. This means that a great deal of acceptance that you are a singular being with two beings that creates all that you desire through sex has to be embraced. Having the will of power and eagerness next to believe in gratitude for what is, will create and produce another being. Therefore this means that, to create, you will have to have sex and understand what you are doing to know what you are creating—

You mean that I should sleep with my opposite, and we will give birth to a being, or simply to put it, a child, right, Parent?

Well you are all-quite-right, but not in the sense of thought that you have, I mean not in a cliché classical conformed norm of having sex, child.

Now be attentive for this is how I mean: Yes you are right, do have sex with your opposite to create. Yet you see my good child, you and your partner just as you will, can have and produce a child or a being without being in contact and physical sexual penetration, because you each have and are male and female as one, already (inside your bodies).

Wait ⋯ so you mean we can have a baby without sleeping together and having intercourse, Parent?

Yes, child.
But how is this all possible though?

It is because it is a dream. A dream is unlimited and everything is possible, can be done and will be achieved as dreamt by using thought imaginatively to create desires from memory. Now listen, oh good great child, for this is how it can be done, and will be done as you choose.

Sex is beautiful. Sex is great. It is the creative beauty that reveals who you think to be, openly secretive. Sex is not particular to anything. You may and can engage in sexual activity with anyone or anything at any time as many times you choose and want, (it really matters not). Yet it is within the nature and purpose of its intention, that you have misunderstood it.

At this moment now, my good child, you have been using sex for the pleasing experience of it, rather of its use. You love the feeling and experience in vain. This simply means that you have quite fallen for the pleasures and synergetic ecstasy that it offers through experience for creation. Having this in mind, you have thus indulged, and without any intention of the outcome, have given birth to a being, without a clear conscious motive of what you are creating and how it will appear, and its purpose of its creation. This is to say that you have a child, yet you do not know what its purpose is, and what it will do, once it is here. And so it is thus apparent; you create a being that is not fully conscious, yet rather confused of its purpose to its current life, from inside of you, to the world outside.

Wow ⋯ yeah, that is actually true. I never thought of it that way, and I still do not know why, Parent.

Yes, like I have told you before that, there is more to sex than you now understand, child.

Yeah⋯ so why is that?
Good. Now listen to what follows.

Now for you to bring forth life with purpose and meaning, through creation to birth; like I have said, you have to acknowledge and accept yourself as a creative being with two. And whatever you create comes from inside of you, even your thoughts, to reality as an object or material. Now then, holding this truth about yourself, before creating a being, and this is to say a child, you should first choose to be clear as to whom with you would love to create. The choice is made through clarity of the one you relate and share the same interests of value with, being it so anyone. Because of mutual concur, both internally and externally, by both respective individuals, the process is then simplified.

Before any encounter or engagement of corporeal sexual intercourse, you and your partner should choose to discuss, know and clarify how, why and what the purpose is, of what you intend to create. A child is a, and is another version of you as you think. You create a child from inside of you to improve yourself, or to better your situation of current life in experience of your desires, with new thoughts. Improvement of yourself concerns living differently entirely, as an entity, from old thoughts of your life (which you are still living right now), as another version. To better or improve current situations of your life now, you then create a child as another version of you, so that it may do what you missed and did not do from all possible opportunities this world offers every day, as so to experience them (as a new person). This is to finally say that you create yourself as many times better as you think, to know yourself concerning your capabilities and power, to experience as you think. A child is you born again.

Now then, once you know and have remembered on the decision of who you are, you then proceed knowing the full outcome of what your thoughts borne from your creative imagination, of what you will both bring to life with your partner, because you are creating yourself. Thereafter, once your created being is in this life, that is to say a child is in this world, you then inform and tell it its purpose by reminding it of what it was created for or to do in this life or world. In this way, it will thus not be confused, nor will it cause it. This is to say that you let it know of what you thought of it, before and when it was created.

Now, yet all of this is truly accomplished by you having a clear choice with the one you love mutually. This is why it is important for you to carefully choose the next person of which you say you relate with to have a ship of love together through sex, because you will be creating with that person. This is the very reason why there is a relationship of love between only two people and not more. It is so because, only two with their love, they will thus create it into being, in expression as a child or whatever it is that is thought. Therefore when choosing a partner, you should know that you are making a choice to create with that person, for that is why you would only sleep and have sex with.

Okay, wow, I do hear you, good Parent.
Good, child.

Now listen for you should choose not to do it. When you have created a child, and you know its purpose and have told it. This does not mean that you have authority over and to it, for in truth you have authority over nothing but yourself, and what you create as a being, is you of part. And this we will discuss shortly after.

Now then, having created a child does not mean that you should boss it around, and dictate its decision, especially in the latter years. A child should only know its purpose and have the will to do as pleases from choice, just as you do now, while bearing in mind its purpose; for should it get lost in the pleasure of creation in this world, It will always go back by remembering, as opposed to being confused and not clear. Also do look to see not to choose to manipulate your creation to have your way; because any decision taken up on your influence for self, will be against you when not producing favorable results for your creation. This is to say that, when a child does not experience and express its full being, which is to create, due to your dictatorial self needs, it will blame you as the creator (just as you blame your parents), because you will be adding more of that which you intended of its purpose in alteration from the original thoughts.

Mm, that is very interesting and deep. I hear you loud and clearly, Parent. But now tell me here. Say that I purposely create a child or a being to solely serve me and do as I command, is that okay? And what should I or be done when it refuses?

Good, very good you are doing child. This is a good question and I love it and, it leads me more closely on how to remind you on how you create.

Yes it is all good and alright for there is nothing that is not. Now you should remember this, whatever you create holds each and every single characteristic of you as whole being. Like we said, you literally replicate yourself. When you have intentionally created a being for such selfish purposes, you should know that it is bound to react as it chooses just as you would, freely. It does this because it holds your features, this is to say that it is able to repudiate, just as you do have a choice to say no.

So then, yes, you can create a being for your purposes and needs, and this is done through a process of wiping or removing a certain neurological memory gene of its brain, by not putting it in its creation process.

Wait ⋯ what? I do not understand Parent.

Ah, do not worry good child, you will understand now, when I explain and tell you how you can create a being without having a standard classical physical sex.

Okay, I believe I am ready for that now, Parent.
All good, now let us begin.

For you to be able to create, you and your partner should know and have the same concept of what will be produced. This means that, thought, mind, body and soul are synchronized and linked the same. There should not be a slight temper or render in the process moment of creation. For any slight change, especially by thought, will alter the initial desired outcome of results. Again, this is to emphasize that before you enter the process of creating what you are conscious of, you should know with whom you will create and that they want and choose the same thing.

Creation of a child or a being without any physical sexual contact encounter is done and achieved through the conscious alert meditative state of sleep, of this current dream of your life. Sleep activates and rouses the experience of thought wholly holistically, from imagination. When you sleep your body goes into an intrinsic mode aroused by desire, curiosity, and love to what the mind searches and seeks to know of its past and future events in experience of it, of this current, for solutions.

Now then, when you and your partner are sleeping, and are both conscious and alert of same linked and synchronized thoughts, you visit each other on the level of same desire; this is to say that you share the same dream through sleep as reality—aware. You will both come together, in a dream, and make love by dissembling, rearranging your bodies, and reconstructing and merging yourselves as desired, forming a whole being, in assistance and agreement, from your aware conscious thoughts in your imagination.

This simply means that you combine two bodies (in small fragmented particles, that shift and change form like liquid), respectively of yours and your partner's, to form one being, according to what you both agree on from your thoughts about it (as you observe it in your sleep) consciously aware, of and in a dream.

Your experiences of this marvelous creation are consciously felt and done within your body, rather than outside. Your body cells interact inherently with each other from the reality of thought that is experienced, and exchanges information as consciously thought by both of you. Semen and virginal fluids are spurt internally throughout the body by each cell, which then gives an extremely overwhelming tinkling pleasure of love full of joy. They create an ecstatic sensation to the body holistically, to every cell of the body, and your brain becomes actively charged. This happens because, visual is deeply concentrated from where the eyes are, to conceptualize the image that is desired, and because every cell is producing. It is exactly sex, yet you totally and extremely feel it inside.

Finally when the link is disconnected, that is to say when you are done and are satisfied of your creation, your female side discharges the exchanged and combined information of characteristics to the womb so that it may develop. This is all possible because you carry both genes of information of a man and woman inside of you, and that it is a dream. Again, you are a whole being with two! Now then, this is how virgins are able to create a being, they do it through a dream.

Wait, you just wait a minute here. So are you tipping and suggesting that this is how the virgin Marry gave birth to Jesus?

Well not only Marry and Jesus particularly as you think now, and assume, yet to all virgins and non-, that have and will. They achieve this in their dream that, they hold account of, consciously. You are created in this fashion as well, yet you do not see it. Remember that I told you on nothing of how you are created and come to being.

Yes I do. Mm ··· okay, I see, Parent.

Now, in context to your question of whether you should create a child for your own selfish needs that follows orders and instructions, and how to go about it. You use and do the same process I have just explained. Yet in the creation process, your thought of it or about it, and that is to say a child, should lack some memory of intellectual will. This is to say you literally create a being that does not think on its own to question authority, yet rather only takes and follows orders.

Okay, so you mean I will basically be creating a stupid dumb being, Parent?

Well not really, for I have told you many times that there is no such as a stupid being, yet it only forgets. And when you create such a being, it means it has no memory of self-will, that is to say it has forgotten and does not remember being able to think and do on its own, for you will have removed such a memory when you created it. And since that it is that, what you create is who you are, you will have then created yourself dumb willingly, and yet have no clue of it because you will have forgotten what you did to yourself.

Mm, oh ··· okay, I see ··· wow. So that is how it is?
Yes it is my good child.

Okay, I see good Parent. I know that was rather a childish question, but I just want to know how things work man. I really just want to know!

And I know ⋯ I know very well my good child. I understand.

Thank you for being who you are, I love you Parent.
And I to you.

Now listen for this is love in attraction for pleasure. Your body reacts to stimulus sensation of touch. Whether touched by a man or woman, anywhere —your body reacts. And if the touch is gentle and soft, brushing over the small hair through skin pores and petals and folds, it consciously alerts and sensually provocatively arouses the entire body' s state. When the whole body is consciously alert, each micro cellular being of you, becomes operational and active, thus hormones are discharged from within and are felt inside the body, which then becomes a great experience, because each part of you is in production and pro-creation; and also from the extrinsic touch. Therefore this means that pleasure is already inside of you, yet it should be awoken or stimulated.

Internal sexual stimulation is caused and can be created when the two beings of the whole, microscopically in cohesion have desire to form themselves newly whole. Each and any released produced substance, travels through small tube veins of tissue muscle to the same store to combine as it vibrates ecstatically along the body because it is full of life. Once when most of released matter reaches one place or store, they become excited to meet and be one; these are kept in the prostate and or testicles and, ovary for production. Since that these store capsules are mainly miscellaneously connected to your external organ, you then feel the sensation taking place. When this process is active from within, a whole being, and that is to say you; feels the experience, then desires to express it with the one you can create with, to bring that feeling out as product. Your feelings then evoke the experience in your mind, which you then see as imagination from within. This then adds to the feeling that you call horny, because you cannot control the great pleasing experience of creation that is going on inside of you, and you just want to take it out.

Sexual attraction and desire to a person, is caused by images, and graphical representation of what you know in consideration of what they can do, concerning flexibility, mobility, size and shape, and firmness, of how you can cope or handle and what you can do to them during sex. Your desire to and of a person is according to what you think of them during, and when you internally have sex with yourself imaginatively. Your external desires are aroused by internal ones. Yet sex is only for creation, and it does not really care much as you think, of how a person is or looks. And any experience of it at any moment, gives the same results of pleasure.

You can get and have pleasure from the least of most persons you would expect, even from a man or woman. With this in mind, it means that you are attracted to the pleasure of sex and not the image of the person, and it can be stimulated by anybody. Yet here now, you have created your own fantasy of what you think is good to you in your own imagination. This is why, even though you are attracted to your current partner by love, yet after having sex or having released from within, your sexual feelings subside. You become enough of that person after that moment, till you start over to feel horny again provocatively by your own internal imaginative thoughts, or external images—(as projected by the ones from inside). This is why sex becomes pointless when you just have sex without discharging or having an orgasm, and cannot go on for great hours; it is so because nothing is being created from within, there is no full desire. Even though you might think that your partner is sexy and hot, yet if you do not feel anything from within, he or she will just be that, as you think, and no attraction of sexual intercourse. You are only attracted to the experience of sex; and to whom and with you have it with, is highly entirely your choice according to what you think is good to you, yet the outcome will be the same when you feel satisfied with anybody or anyone and or eve anything—at any given moment.

Now then, the war is over when you agree individually with the two beings inside of you, according to their desires. This process is achieved when you have understood relationship. Explicitly, the two beings are relatives of the one that they are. They relate to each other. You have to come to a great understanding that a woman relates to and with a man. Therefore you have to choose to agree and accept that a woman is attracted to a man, and a man to woman, it is a relationship (of relatives or relativity). It is so, as so they may create themselves, and understand. You have a choice to sleep and have sex with anybody at any time, as long as you both mutually utterly agree. Mutual agreement can either be the same or different, this is to say that you can agree on different things or the same. You have to agree that a great part of you loves men, and a great part of you loves women, else otherwise you would not communicate to relate with either of any. The relation of and on how you will experience yourself, either opposite or the same, is weighed dependently on your feelings about what and who you are. When you have and feel great desire to be with women—because you love them, you will do so because you are relating greatly with that part of yourself. Because relationship is full of love, yet what you do will determine your experience of the relationship with women.

Therefore in a relation with and to a woman, when you also along with all the great inclusive things a relationship has to offer, you enjoy sexual intercourse as a man with women, it is okay because you relate through sex, to understand yourself (as that part—a woman). This is why as a man you have and do encounter a few of many different relationships with woman through sex—it is so because you are relating to the other one of yourself of the whole, through pleasure by feeling each other. And any one of all the women there are, is a part of a man that you are. The same is said for the man side part of you. You encounter few of many men through sex relation, because that is how you relate with a man. And any one of all the men there are, is a part of a woman that you are.

Yet I tell you this; sex is not the only method and manner of relation to each other to yourself. A relationship includes communication of and through words, enjoyment of nature and materialistic things with the person you would love to spend any moment with. And any moment from a second, can be spent with either a man or a woman, doing what you love and enjoy, with him or her.

Now with this truth, it means that you can and may enjoy spending time with men, and do all the fun things they do, because you share the same interest, and that is why you relate to them, yet you do not have a sexual relation with them but rather with women, because you do not feel them that way, and yet this does not mean they cannot stimulate, arouse or sexually please you. And you may also on the other hand, enjoy the things that women do, yet you do not have a sexual relation with them but rather with men, because you do not feel them that way, yet this does not mean they cannot stimulate or sexually please you. The same way you relate to one is the same way you relate to the other one.

Anything and everything that you do with anyone, whether you like or hate them, the things that you do together will cause you to relate at that moment of doing and being, and that is what brings you together in that ship; which is a relationship (of relativity), and you create and do whatever you want from thought to material, through sex or mere company, or manipulation of matter for materialism. Therefore, my great beautiful child, relationship is to relate. You have to understand this in order for the war inside of you to stop. This is to say ultimately say that, love yourself wholly and completely.

Now I tell you this my lovely. The war will stop once you stop fighting that man, and the war will stop once you stop fighting that woman. At this moment, because of refusing and failing to understand that you are in a relationship with yourself as one whole with two beings; you are still fighting for power as either a man or a woman. Instead of sharing it, to be that which you desire together—rather, you choose to have one dominate the other opposite half of the same self, (one body), in claim of superiority. You my child, especially you—you infuriate your opposite and demean it. This you do and achieve through judgment of your past mistakes that are done by the other, currently.

Rather than understanding, just as you have progressed to where you are now, to lead yourself together, that is to say this one great awesome body of yours to a greater self as whole, you choose to have and make your opposite less, concerning how it thinks and does things, from your understanding of past things that you yourself did that you now see and highly think are not good, unfit, productive or progressive to where you choose and want to lead and direct your human body to.

With this power hungry motive mind, you then fight to be a better woman than a man, and after defeating the man you are, you then fight the woman to be a better man that does not get defeated by woman. You keep on redistributing and recycling power between yourself. And now I tell you this, choose to hold hands together and raise them up to show your power as one and, you shall see that the war will stop. Choose to rule no other but yourself, and you shall have peace the way you want it. Choose love above all to yourself as whole together, man and woman as you are already, and you shall have peace. Choose you as a whole being with two, and understand, and you shall have peace. And like I said, this is all possible when you both agree, in this dream.

Mm, I now understand who I am. Thank you, I appreciate it and I love you.

And I to you.

FREE-LOVE-LAW

This is what love says

Freedom is who you are. Will and liberation in alpha creation and omega existence is your definitive truth. Oh great child, the one born and created without any rules or exceptions. The one that wills self accordingly to be anything of desire without peripheral control of manipulation, you are free. Oh beautiful smile of will—fiercely untamed as the sun and full of dazzling rapture that glint from eyes—you are free!

Now, listen. You are free as the void of the universe, because of that the universe is not prisoned or bound and or restricted by anything, and it is creation itself, and you are made from it, you are therefore thus liberated good child. This being so, it means that there is only one law that holds and binds you, and it is your own self-created law. Anything and everything that you wish and want to do, can and will be done as long as it abides by or to your rule and law.

Yes, there is only one law, and it is your free love law. It is the only one law, because it is only for you, and because there is only one of a kind of you. You have this rule of law—that you have created, because it is who you truly are naturally, without any modification and state change of being, and because it selfishly serves you and, meets your desires and what you want from perceptual imagination. Your free-love-law consists of morals of self, which in turn creates desires to be experienced and serve you alone in love, selfishly.

Mm ⋯ selfishly, how do you mean, Parent, I am not sure if I am getting all of this?

Well, I know that you strongly think and feel that being selfish is a bad thing, especially as compared to being selfless, child, yet I promise you as you have assured yourself through experiences, that, complete selfishness creates selfless.

Okay, you know I am keenly listening, Parent.

Good, now listen to what follows, for again it is great wisdom of your truth in your knowledge.

Everything that you have done, you have done it selfishly to satisfy your desires that you so much love to experience in the moment. You are hungry, and you eat to keep and maintain good health for yourself for fulfillment, selfishly. You have sex to satisfy yourself desires, selfishly. You buy, pamper and spoil yourself with luxury, selfishly. You solve and create new ideas for your own benefits to be uniquely smart and intelligent, selfishly. The list goes on of the things that you do to and for yourself selfishly in love of. This is because you are here for your own experience, and no one else's but yours.

Now, it is only after, when you are satisfied with what you have had or done in experience of it, you then become selfless by giving what you have had or done to someone. After being full, pleased, spoiled, intelligent, you then want to give to another person what you have as so they may experience it as well the way you have. This is to simply say that, after completing your selfish desires, you then become selfless—yet only after you.

Mm ⋯ I see what you mean, good Parent. And well, I will say that it is actually true in my life. I mean I honestly do not remember giving someone something I have not had or used before. Come to think of it, I don't think that I can give what I have not owned before.

124

Now, here it is again, child. Therefore when you are completely selfish, you will then be completely selfless. This is the reason why a complete selfless person gives everything and rarely-barely ever asks anything because they are satisfied. They are pleased and are enough of most of the worldly materials. Even when they do ask for something, it is to help the other person. And it is within this great selfless act that makes them change the world and become great impactful beings of not only one but, many generations of all time.

At this moment in time of reading this, you have not completely satisfied your self-desires in life, because you still have plans to do, which you think you have not met or accomplished fully, thus you will and still are selfish. You still have a lot to do and acquire in life now, more especially, the things that you have had before, because you are not satisfied with using or having them. You just want more and more of them, many times in different ways and places, good child.

Well I have to say this: greatness and nobility will have to wait just a second, because I am seriously not done. I am going to enjoy being selfish for a while, Parent.

That is very good child. You are doing it for good-self. You are doing good! Thanks Parent.

Oh, by the way, thank you for coming clean and being honest that you will be selfish, child. Through your life you have been denying that you are selfish and only mostly been referring to some others by pointing fingers that they are selfish. So thumbs up to you, you are doing good. And how are you doing now, child?

I am doing good, Parent.
Nah, nah, nah ⋯ let me repeat it again. How are you doing now, child?!

125

I am doing ⋯ Good!

There you go, you have it. Well done! Celebrate.

Oh please, you making me blush, just stop flattering me, just stop it. I don't want to smirk like am already right now. So please, can we get back on it.

Alright then, I am on it, let me hit it!

Move afloat in tranquil through space, brushing the rough ground terrain as the wind of pristine air that flickers dust and is not confined, for that is who you are. Flow as the stream and replenish every moment you are at with roses made of feathers of an eagle that roams the sky freely, for again, that is who are. Now listen, oh good one, for this concerns your own law of freedom.

As a being that you are; that creates things and anything from imagination to express oneself—you created a world of a place full of unlimited possibilities whereby you can, as you may, by will; be, do and have anything that you want and wish, with many others of alike—with you. A world where you can and are able to recreate yourself through sex with those of alike, with you, and give yourself many different names and appearances; a world where vegetation grows and can be eaten; where resources of matter can be molded and changed to be transformed into anything; and where there is unlimited water that recycles itself and creates spectacular spectrum of colors in variation from its own prism that layers transparently around and emits scents of great fumes that freshens and puts mind to tranquility.

This beautiful world that you have created through imagination and have chosen to experience, you thus gave it no law or rule to govern it, for to do so, that would mean there are, and, would be things you should not do when wanting to. You lived with yourself in love and harmony. Domesticated, grew and ate food. Created things as far-off as your imagination is able to conceive —till to this point, to have tools and resources that show your creativeness.

You settled for and, on this lovely orb. Admired, awed and appreciated it for what it is as you have imagined it to creation for its beauty. You enjoyed living on it (as you still do), wandered and loafed it very passionately; and also drinking and eating from it with a very slow relaxed indulgent life of living.

Now then; it is only when you put to reality and, noticed by realizing (being aware) that you like what others—(who are exactly of alike with you in all respective ways), have created for themselves, that you started to want, wish and desired to have exactly what they have and have created for themselves through their imagination and efforts. Instead of creating it yourself, you sought and resorted to asking others to have it created and done for you. Well of course, some did not mind to, because they loved to and it really did please them to give what they love to others, when they asked for it. Yet, while some others did mind, because they know that you are just as much capable just as they are, to do what they have done (in your imagination!)

On various numerous unmentionable occasions of time; to the ones who would not give you what you want and wish, and, think that you cannot create from your imagination, you then took it without their knowledge into your own possession. This, of which then, on their finding, created and caused tension of conflict, and fights of quarrels between and among you as yourselves. This behavior of just taking and not creating for your own-self— you got used to it. Now then, because there was and still is violence over what the other has, you then strategically came up with another great idea.

You very much creatively and imaginatively, again, thought and had a brilliant idea of having laws and rules that enables you to share, trade and have what others have, without fighting over it, yet rather on utter agreement, because you also want it for yourself in love of it, from liking it. And so it is thus as such that, you created your free-love-law of the things you want, that others have created.

Your free-love-self-law is constituted by a set of moral believes and rules that only serve you. These rules of morals you have thus strongly recognized and identified them as so you may not preclude and thwart yourself from being who you are and what you want to freely do and be. You have laid down deep in your conscious heart that, no one shall, and should not steal from you, for should it be so, you will retaliate in vengeance of fight to claim back what is taken. You have laid another rule from your own feelings about it that, no any other should openly or covertly perverse sexually consensually with a partner that you have concurred to relate with, for should it be so, you will retaliate in vengeance of fight to claim back what is taken or even disown your partner, and or take any life involved in the matter, even if it is yours.

On the contrary of taking a life, whether yours or another's, you have yet again laid another rule that, no one shall and should not kill you for any just or unjust reason, for should it be so, you will retaliate in vengeance of fight to claim back what is taken, even after death. These are as is, what defines your moral conscious free-love-self-law. You have put them into place, because you want to express yourself freely as you love and experience things selfishly. With this magnificent truth of your law, this is why you do not want things stolen from you, or a partner cheating on you, or someone or somebody to kill you because; you want something selfishly for yourself only (in this moment), thus it is to you that it should not be taken or stolen or enjoyed.

It is because you want someone to love only you alone selfishly, thus it is to you that they should not sleep around with many others openly or indiscreet secretly. It is because you selfishly want to live and die by self-influenced choice, thus it is to you that no one should harm or kill you. These are your own rules (no one else's but yours). You have made them up from what you feel is right and serves you accordingly individually and selfishly. This is thus as such that you have made a law of morals on yourself rooted deep to the core heart of consciousness that, you will not steal, kill, nor openly or covertly indulge in perverted activities with someone else's partner even though you wish to do so, by trying so hard to controlling your actions and feelings. Therefor this means that, you have based your laws on your feelings about things that act as delimiters or an impediment that does not progressively set you free from doing other things that you desire selfishly.

Mm ⋯ wow, I hear you Parent. But now tell me here dearest, if I am born free as you say I am, and I can do whatever I want, then why do I make up these laws, I mean why should I have and feel that it is necessary to have a law or rules that governs, as free as I am already, even though they were not there to begin with?

Yes my angel of a child, it is because your definition of freedom does not serve you now in favor. Thus you see it good for you, to have a law.

Wait ⋯ what?! Being free does not serve me?

Yes it does not serve you, (yet only not in favor to you). This is so because you saw from a very child young age that you are, as you still see now, that your very own actions reflect towards you. At the age of a baby or a child, you strongly observed and noted that when you hit another, intently or not, it is inevitable, no matter how long it takes that, that other or another will hit you back. You hit because you are free to do so out of your own will of choice. At the age of a baby or a child, you strongly observed and noted that when you steal or take things of others, intently or not, it is inevitable, no matter how long it takes, that others will steal from you to take and claim back. You steal and take because you are free to do so, out of your own will of choice. When a teenager and matured, you strongly observed and noted that when you love someone else's companion partner, intently or not, it is inevitable that, someone else other will, and still does even now, love your companion partner too. You love anything and anyone because you are free to do so by your will.

Finally after understanding that freedom does not have limits, and that it does not have to be portrayed negatively, (and that is to say in way that is not in favor to you) to protect, and not harm or impinge on you, as so you may have your self-desires. You saw and took a great note that you acted carless and were not conscientious with freedom, and you were harming yourself and, in a way you were doing things literally to yourself, thus it did not favor you— which then you made laws that could and will favor you, as a reminder to have all good, and be gentle to yourself.

Mm, I see, Parent.

Now, unbound your subliminal chains from flesh, emancipate yourself, and be present in soul and spirit for I am telling you about freedom. Yes freedom does exist, and is pleasurably indulgent for its expressed creation. Creation is the only ultimate freedom there is in of the universe, and you as part of it, are very much capable to do so. Without the ability to create, there would be no freedom because nothing can or will be produced, made or done, due to the limitation, constraints and restriction. To do or be something, one uses inherent creation of self to produce desired results, as thought from imagination in memory. Therefore this is to emphasize that, freedom is experienced from having to create.

Whatever it is that you want, you can by will, create it. Yet you have limited this ability, thus you have limited your freedom. This limitation and lack of some things, you have lived and produced it through disbelieve in yourself; dependency and laziness.

Firstly on believe: There are many great things of which you think you cannot do or create, especially to specific quality. Since that you believe so, (yet on the contrary you believe that someone can), you then take your freedom of creation and give it to someone else. Well of course this lack of self-believe arose pragmatically from doing things that you did not entirely love that you have seen others do, of which you developed interest in, from liking them.

When you saw that you could not do or create beautifully, just as the one you copied from or espier to be, perfectly, you then give up by demeaning your standard by whipping and beating yourself down with harsh words of such as "I really can' t do this." Yet with all of this lack of self-believe and worthiness, deep down in your heart of consciousness, you know that when you practice and focus on it—you do get and, be better at it, even when you do not love it. Thus you even know and say with your own words that "Practice makes perfect." This statement of yours is very true because you already know that you can when you really want to, because you know everything and are intelligent!

Mm ⋯ well okay, I hear Parent. I hear you loud and clear.
Good, very good you are.

Now secondly on dependency: You have solely depended on others to acquire and have what you think you need and desire. Right here on this very subject, this is to say that you expect people to do things for you. In this you thus give away your very own will, that of which is free (and are born with), of having to do something, to someone else. This then limits your freedom to do or have it even though you can do it, because you wait and depend outside of yourself from and to someone else. This is the very reason why you do not have some things, and have not done or achieved them because you have allowed and disabled your ability of it being so, to the dependency of the other.

Thirdly on laziness: You do not want, and will not to get your hands dirty on the actual work. There are many things of which you want and desire, yet because you have gotten very much used to the idea of having to buy or purchase someone' s creation, it then becomes difficult most of times, to have or acquire it because, you wait a long bit while, to accumulate money as so you may buy it. Yet when you really give time and attention for what you want, you would remember how to make it, by learning, and then create or re-create it yourself to your own specification and want.

Because of that most of the time, you think that there is a lot of work involved in the process learning and developing, to produce, you then shirk, procrastinate in hesitation, and then eventually are just too lazy do it at all, even if it is what you want. So then it has thus been evident that, you rather wait, sometimes, a few odd more years to buy and have what you can create. When you should have spent a year remembering by learning what you want to have from your own memory of intelligence, you rather spend a year saving to have it once, and give the money to the next. You do this because you are too lazy to get it done, and are keeping busy with what you do not even enjoy.

Now I tell you this oh good one. When you believe that you can, and are not lazy, and depending not on to anyone, you will create all that you wish, and will be free as the universe. I tell you this, you will want that house, and you will build it with your own bare hands from your creative imagination. You would want food, and you will plough, plant and grow them with your own hands from your imaginative memory. This creative process goes for everything: clothes, money, cars, and etc. Well of course you only have to remember that you are a whole creative being of two, that can create everything and anything!

Now, because of having not to believe in yourself, depending and looking mostly on to others, and by being lazy to create your own, you then experience lack. Having seeing what is in sight, and believing that you do not have, you then again break the very same laws that you observed and set into place into your daily life, that will favor you. You start to steel, lie, cheat by taking other peoples companions and even contemplate or commit murder even by suicide. Of course, when such thoughts leading to behavior, start to cloud your mind, you forget your own law and what you say you will do, for should you do any of that. This is thus as such that you end up being killed or murdered, locked in prison, shamed and ridiculed in vengeance of your action. This is because you are not aware that what you do on to others, you are doing it to yourself, and are breaking the very law you have set and put into place—that you said you would not have the experience done to you.

And now I tell you this: because that, most of what you want has already been created, all you should do is to create abundant wealth for yourself, by having one great idea—of which you already have (that you love), whether using the tools and resources in your exposal or having create it from scratch, that will multiply and recycle money for you, and then execute it no matter what, in the fashionable way of doing it out of love, through your self-aware talent or talents. Do this, and you shall see the freedom that you have always had, and should have been living from long—to begin with!

Mm ⋯ okay! I hear you, great Parent. And so I shall with all this knowledge presented before me.

Good, very good it is!

IMAGINATION

This is what love says

Be with calm, still and enduring patience. Be whole heartedly here my beautiful one, for I am giving you divine realization and wisdom. This is your latter creation in completion.

Now here is your truth. Whatever it is that you see, even by thought is an image. This means that everything in the universe is an image, or a picture as you would have it formally preferred, child. By any means of all possible realities of creation, nothing can ever be to existence without having a clear complete image or picture of itself distinctively individually or as a collection or a group—and yet the image of the concept exist as seen. With this truth therefore it means that imagination is the first to last result of creation. There is nothing you can achieve, do or be, without seeing it as an image. In order to do or be anything in particular, you first have to see it as a picture—without this, it will not be realized and, that is to say made to reality or achieved. Imagination is relived and re-created through a divine wonderful process experience of thought mechanism and of sex, to be experienced.

First and far most, sex creates everything, because of desire to become an image of type that is seen and desired, that already exists. When two beings or particles, just as you are, bond together, they produce a certain image of themselves as desired.

Thought is the process mechanism to choice in the moment of prayer, of who you are. This simply means that anything that is accumulated and acquired is had by thorough thinking, to select options that resemble experience of desire and, identifies who you are. Thought is the selection process of prayer to all the available (already existing) options of creation in a dream.

Creation is complete, and it only forms, molds and changes itself uniquely as a whole to a certain particular image it desires as an entity. Creation is beautiful, and is such a great awe to admire, and thus it is the ultimate image.

Wow ⋯ I do understand that, parent, and that' s why I let you go on and did not interrupt.

Good. Now, to clarify that all is an image, I have to make you realize this truth as well, child. Whenever and whatever you think, you think in images, that is to say pictures. This means that even words before uttered, are thought and seen as images.

What! Words are pictures, Parent?

Yes they are. A word consists of letters of alphabets. An alphabet is an image as and of a particular form and, is assigned meaning to. A combination of alphabets creates a word picture that is assigned to a particular object to uniquely identify it, as that image. When voice of sound is uttered, it vibrates travelling through space and, is received or interpreted and converted to an image, and or a picture to its assigned object, by the recipient, which in this case (the recipient) is you.

Uttered words of voice from sound, without being assigned or linked to an image, make no sense at all. They make no sense because there is no referential picture or image of its existence in your memory of dream, which in turn creates the unknown. This is one of the main reasons why when you encounter a new, unfamiliar or none existing word, in your memory, you become confused and not clear of what it is or means. It is so because there is no created image of it in your mind. Therefore this thus stresses that to understand, know and see something, it has to be an image, otherwise it does as it will not, exist. Right now my very good child, you are experiencing and living the image of creation—(you are the image).

I am? How, my good Parent?
Pay attention to what follows, child.

Now, remember I said that a being as you are consists of only creation, and creation consists of only a polarity that repels itself to a different flow of movement and form, to create itself as duality and or even multiples. This simply means that creation clones itself, thus creates an image of itself to know itself.

At this moment, my very sweet good precious child, you are experiencing the image of creation in an opposite flow direction of movement. Remember also that, creation is complete, which means there is nothing missing in creation, the image is complete and done. Now when I said that, you are experiencing the image of creation in an opposite direction—in stressing, I meant that you are experiencing yourself as you are already as a complete image. Since creation is complete, you are living the process of it now in the unified moment, therefore not adding anything, but living the complete experience of it. Also since you are experiencing the process of creation of what you are and what it is, it means that you can as you will, reverse the process back the opposite direction and live as creation and, not the process of creation. You are an individual part inside the image of creation of the wholly universal being, of dream.

Now, listen to this. For you to reverse the process, and understand it, this is what you should choose to remember first. A thought is a selection process of choice to an image. This simply means that, you cannot, and will not think, if there is no image or "picture" of what you know, created in your conscious mind. You would have no choice because there is no option of an image of a particular thing to choose from, and select. An image is complete creation. And also again, this simply means that an image is what already exists. Sex is re-productive process to re-experience an image. This is to say that sex is therefore, the experience of an image that re-produces it by re-creation.

Now, these are what define creation. You can call them, only as you wish – the holy three, the great three or the mighty three, or the whatsoever trinity. Call them whatever you want as you may in any order you will. So now, the first is: image of creation that already exist, followed by thought process to make a choice; which is also followed after by sex, to re-experience the choice process made by thought from an image. They are simply as follows:

- Image—(existence)
- Thought—(Choice)
- Sex—(Pro-creation, and or to produce)

All is possible. Now listen oh good one. Every time when you see and imagine anything, know that it is done. Therefor this is to say that, with the power of imagination that exists already in the universe embedded in your mind, you can have and be all you want from your imagination. This glorious profound divine truth is achieved by knowing and accepting that when you imagine something you can as it is, be. When this truth is carried along with, all the time, you will then be able to imagine and be whatever you say you are just by thinking and uttering words, and then by being in deed, in the moment of it. This is so because your words affirm and confirm to your thoughts about an image that you see, that is in the universe imbedded in your mind.

Wait ⋯ hold on here just for a moment; so you are saying that I can just simply think something and say it, and then I will just be it, instantly, Parent?

Well you know me my honey child of universe that, nothing has been impossible with me.

Okay, I am rich ⋯ right now ⋯ Hum, I do not see any changes, why, Parent? Why is everything still the same ⋯ where is my wealth? You just said that if I think and say, I will be, so you are basically lying to me and making a fool out of me!

Like I always say my all-star child, I will not lie nor fool you, for doing so is lying and fooling myself that I have fooled you, and that, I will not do. All you have to do is listen to what I say, and choose (think) how you will carry your dream.

Well you know me Parent that, I am just waiting on you to explain this bizarre phenomenal way of life and perspective to me. And I am already guessing that you have some valid points from what you have given to me so far at this point. So how is it possible?

Well you see, you are only starting to remember now, yet not of full capacity, but, are surely moving there. Meaning that you have not given yourself time to be capable and able to do this now at this moment, yet I will tell you how it is done.

Okay cool.
Now listen to what follows.

Yes my treasure, just by imagining and choosing by thought, and then affirming by word or deed, you can as you will and as you are now, be anything. Now here is what has been the main major impediment for you to achieve this instant result of it, and that is: forgetting. Again, you forget because you ignore what you do not want or what you think is not of necessity or value to you. This of course, meaning that you do not care of or about it in this or at that moment, child. Now, with this choice of willing forgetfulness, you have then thus dissipated and blurred some events, places and things that you do not consider important, even though you use them and are present at the place of the occurring event in the moment; you still choose to as you are now, to not hold and grasp the image of what is happening around you clearly.

Well of course so that you may understand, this means that: you find yourself doing something, and or are at some place, yet you cannot identify what you were busy with to precision, or the place you were at clearly. To even stress this point, you are yet still not able to descriptively imagine yourself of how you look. You are not able to create an image of yourself of how you look and are in your imagination. The image is there, yet you cannot see it clearly. You also have been passing the same vagrant on the same street almost every day, yet you cannot create and see the proper image of that person of how he or she looks, from your imagination when they are not in your presence. This goes for buildings, signs, street-names, people and objects in their variety. You even shock yourself and are stupefied, that you were not aware that a particular thing was or is where it is now, yet all this time you did not know that. This is again of that, you are ignorant and, choose to be by your own will!

Wait, what?! So I am supposed to know everything?
No you do not, child, only what you choose, remember?

Yes I do, good Parent.

Now that we are done with forgetting; this is why you are not producing or creating instant results by word from thought of an image. It is so because, when you say something from word, you are not clear of how it looks even if and when you know. So, just like you said that you are rich, which yes indeed you are very rich, yet you are not clear on this, and that is to say that you have doubt. Your doubt arises from the current clear image that you see from self-made choices, of the situation and condition you are in now, in this moment, which is lack of something in desire of it, and or poverty—the image of this fact, is real to you. And yet again, you create a blur uncertain image in your mind of being rich, and then perceive a clear image of you being poor or lacking something in your reality. Now with this soul quenching truth in mind, words are not made real because the image they espier to be in desire, is not clear, thus they just echo and fade into the present perceived reality that is known and clearly seen, which is poverty and lack, without producing results.

Your mind holds two truths, of which the first is an unclear image of what you want and desire, and followed by the second, which is what you are really seeing right now, in sight, in your reality. It struggles and battles with itself in deep cogitated concentration of what is, and then makes a choice from what it really sees from the current perceived moment. So for words to produce the seen image that is wanted and desired instantly, from mental, they rely on its clarity, and that is to say crystal clear just as you see and read these words right now.

Wow, I hum ⋯ I ⋯ I must say I really did not know that, Parent. I really did not think of it in that way, at least I should say! Wow that is just amazing! So all I have to do is to see the image clearly, Parent?

Yes, and that is all.
Okay, I am with you, I got you on that, Parent.

Now, not only have you not consciously been unable to create a clear image in your mind to be manifested in your reality, yet and also, you have conversely consciously created and seen clear images of what you want in life concerning your dream, but have ignored them due to your current perceived image in sight, and thus you have produced what you do not want.

Okay, slow it down a bit there, Parent ⋯ meaning?

This means that just as you are not ultimately able to consciously descriptively detail and see a picture of things of past moments, current, present or future, by creating them as they are in your imagination, to experience them now in your reality. You are also consciously seeing and creating what you see and know from your imagination, to reflect on your reality. In a simplified and amplified understanding, this is to say that you are unconscious and conscious. You have based your reality on this paradoxical creation ⋯ Please bear with me child, for I am trying as much hard as possible to make and help you understand this by re-iterating words. I can feel you are a bit edgy and confused there.

Okay, no it's cool. No problem, Parent. Well I guess you know me very well hey?

Yes I do my special one. Yes I do.

Now this is how you have done it and are doing it, child. You have previously successfully created, incredibly enduringly orchestrated and have done things and allowed them to exist in your now reality, even though you did not fully want their experience in your life. This you have thus achieved through the process of images in your mind to reality. This is to graciously ultimately say that, even when you know, even when you do have a clear picture from your imagination and are aware of who you do not want to be, or what you do not want to do in life, you still do it because that is what you only see and say in your imagination of memory, rather than seeing who you are. Since that the mind holistically sees this image, of who you are not, most if not all the time, it then surrounds your space environment with that image and more of it.

Now I tell you this as a reminder. During your educational school attendance, you do some activities and even pass some subjects significantly to a degree, even though that you utterly ultimately clearly know that you do not want to do or be any of that, of those disliked subjects, yet you still did. These of course then accumulate a pile of who you are not, leaving the very exact traces of that, of you in definition. You also go to what you call work without desire to, even when you know by head and heart that, that is not the picture of who you are, or what you really want to be in this now life. These of course then accumulate a pile of who you are not, leaving the very exact traces of that, of you in definition. This again, is so because you think, and then say it, which then brings it to life, by only knowing and seeing the same picture of who you are not every day when you sleep and wake up to it, in your dream by being.

This was and is all possible because you only knew who you were not, and were just as you are now, still trying to figure out who you truly are in this big dream of yours. You are conscious of who you are not, and you are unconscious of who you are. Conscious and unconscious!

Mm ··· wow! I understand. I am listening and I do hear you, Parent.
Well, what do we say, child?

Something like ··· "good, very good!"
And there you go, child.

Now listen, the one that I pride myself with. Bring yourself together for I am giving you the answer. This is again the great divine without terms other than of yours. This is the treasure of created images of that are creation, therefore seek to grasp just as you have found its meaning on these words, here.

Images create reality. Once an image is perceived and conceived, it is just that, and nothing else. This means that you can have a clear image of who you want to be, and what you want to do in life, and be very successful at creating it as a reality of your dream by living it, and it will just be that and nothing else. It will be just an image of who you are. Therefore the only thing that gives an image an experience is, feeling ··· yes, feeling! This is so because without feeling, you would have a creation of something particular, yet you would not know how it feels because you do not have emotions or feeling. In your own words, this would make sense by saying that you will be like a "robot" . An image and, with emotions of feeling create experience. Since that an image is who and what you think you are, this means that you and feelings create experiences. The two coexist concentrically together in harmonious peace.

Mm ⋯ wow, I see. This is great news, Parent.

It is so because you are feeling it, thus it is an experience, otherwise it would just be written images of words, and there would be no holy moment of this now time—in experience of it.

Wow I do get it. Yes I really do understand, thank you!

You are welcomed, my sparkling diamond shining on the surface of the free flowing river reflecting the sun as it glints.

Mm, I like that, it sounds nice, Parent.
Do you want more?

Nah, I am good, please, carry on, I am still listening.

Now I tell you this: Yes you can be anything you want and have anything you want, just as you have allowed and accepted your current condition and situation to take place for now, until you have decided on the next move that you know will be successful and, have made a choice of who you are. Yet the success of having created what you want and who you are, is determined by feeling; your feelings about it.

This means that you may have been the person you want to be and, what you have always wanted to be and do in life, yet it is not bringing you the success, and especially concerning the riches and wealth you had hoped on. This is so because of feeling. Even though you have chosen your dream clearly from the images that you see of yourself and are living it, your fluctuating feelings determine its success. Any feeling within any moment of your dream now, will either take or give more success to you and—, either of any positive or negative that is great, will be your experience of your dream. Therefor this means that you may be and have what you want, yet because of any dreary day to your dream, you thus give that and take or degrade its success.

These feelings that take from the success of your dream are mainly caused by what you influence and accept in your life situations. Your negligence and recklessness behavior of the image that you portray negatively, and that is to say opposite, off from the image you are, is the influence, that gives exactly negatively opposite feelings to your dream; feelings that come from the judgment of others about you, which in turn you tend to accept and have them as your own. And finally, just when you have had enough of what others think and say of you; you then bounce back their feelings about you, by acting and saying that you do not care, and it does not matter what they think and say about you. This of course then impinges on your dream, because of the reason that you are breaking your very own law of showing care to your dream, and are changing the rules again. Thus as such that the people whom you presented yourself to, to offer your talent of skill in your dream, then look back away, and thus take their support and love away from you, that they had given prior in love, because they are now not impressed with the image they see insight before them, that you portray from or in your dream in this life!

Mm ··· wow! Please carry on, I am listening, Parent.

Good! So then, whenever you do something that you love, and have always wanted to be, and are feeling a low negative emotion at any moment of doing it on a day, it will not be successful because of how you are feeling at that moment of doing it due to your feelings! Therefore this means that, the longer you have sad, acrimonious moments of any external factors not of the cause of your dream, for as mostly as long in your dream, you will not be successful even when doing who you are, what you love, and your dream! You also know this very well, my good child. There have been days when you have not done best on the thing that you love, and you normally give this excuse as a rational reason: "I was having a bad day," and or, "I was not feeling good" and or even "I just didn' t feel like it."

Yep, you are right. Yes indeed you are right Parent. So now tell me, what should be done to make my dream successful?

Well we both know that the answer to that is very simple, my good child.
Yes, again you are right, Parent.

Yes, as we both know, the answer is happiness. When you have happy feelings, you create success to your dream. The more-happier you feel, the more successful you get. And the more-happier merrier you get, the more-greater success and wealth you get to your dream! Happiness and joy, affirms that all is going well. And I mean exactly that, all is going well!

Okay, I hear you. So all I have to do and be is to be happy all the time?

Well that would be advantageously a very great thing for you, child.
Is it a must, do I have to, and how do I be happy all the time anyway, Parent?

Again the choice is yours. And as for telling you how to create happiness, is beyond the scope of this conversation of text between me and you, child.

So you will not tell me, Parent?
Well not now, my lovely.

Okay, are you really not going to tell me? Do you know who I am? I mean do you really know who you dealing with right now? Do you have any idea! I got people, and they know people, if you don't tell me right now—

Whoa ⋯ I am starting to have a picture ⋯ jeez okay, okay. I will give you a head start. Just calm yourself, child. Well, you can just start by simply saying that "I am now happy," and then laugh at yourself after saying that. You will see that you will be happy.

Are you making fun of me, Parent? And by the way, that actually sounds and seems crazy.

Well, I did my job. Now, back to serious stuff!

Now at this moment, my diamond child, you have only achieved a small fraction of whom and what you say you want and choose to be by a small fraction of instantaneous results. This is to say that you have only been thinking within the range of your daily reality, of the things that you already know that you should or need to do. This routine of yours has depicted an image on your mind of what it should produce, from the same choices of every day. This is why you can create, and have easily small things such as food, money, clothes and etc. quickly before the sunsets. This is so because, it is what you only mostly think; you only see these images of small things that you want daily, thus as such you are living it, as the image seen in your imagination (to outside).

Yet when you are willing, and had you expanded your mind to and for what you want, through all other optional universal pleasures, glory and desires, you would have them now just as you have what you want daily (even what you do not want by thinking of them consistently perpetual! Yet again because you are happy with what you have, you then have more of it many times daily, in different ways, and in different quantities of more or less of the same, in abundance! This form of short narrow continuous thinking then, makes it hard and difficult for you,(as you would say), to have what you desire because you do not think, see, do and be, everyday often just as you would with your activities that you think you need to survive on—daily.

Wow, so it is that simple, Parent?
Yes it is that easy. It is that simple and it is that great. Just imagine!

Okay, I think and believe that—I understand that and I got it.
Good!

DREAMS

This is what love says

Oh my sweet dreamer—the one and only dreamer that has flooded oceans with dreams of tranquility harmoniously to the sweet and melodious sounds of creation to perfection of love by pure awesomeness. The one that has seasoned and sprinkled thoughts through imagination, that which give good indulgent flavored aromas of the scattered universe in your dream. You are a true divine sparkling reality of creation in motion by thought and being, by your own imagination. You are the great legendary dreamer of all unified time and there is no one like you in the whole entire universe, for you are the universe.

In the beginning of this dream, there was and still is, you. A vision that is so vividly great and beautiful was created, by you. You closed your eyes and created marvelous and awesome wonders of your present moment in your imagination. When you opened your eyes, to see this beautiful creation of yours; you saw beautiful people, animals, plants and oceans of water that are of, with and against each of one other in good and or bad for love, on this great rock full of sand and water. You saw a place full of life and of your creation. You saw vehicles that fly through the sky, and vehicles that move and scrape on the earth: A place full of your information that moved everywhere and anywhere within seconds between devised devices. You blinked and looked again, and saw lights around in space that shine, glow and twinkles the great void—giving a spark that ignites great infinite possibilities, and moving beautifully about to show their magnificence and meaning in your dream according to you as you have willed it, by desire. And this is what you said: "I love it. I really do love it, and it is so beautiful."

I am here fully in soul. I am present with all my heart and being. My attention is devoted to feel, hear and listen eagerly as so to be, with excitement for what you have to say. I am so happy, I am grateful beyond spoken words. Wow, I am really glad that we are finally talking about dreams. I mean this is what I have been waiting on, and this is what I have lacked to fully understand in my entire existence. I have been confused by my dream. I did not know what caused my dream and where it was, and also not to mention how to move and get to it. It took me a great deal of my existing time to come to this point of how a dream works and what it is, Parent.

Wow ⋯ you really poured out all your heart there, child. I mean you really could not wait to get to this point.

Yes, you know this, Parent. I mean if I really do understand what dreams are, then I will sleep and wake merrily beautiful. I will not fear, be uncertain, bewildered, nor will I doubt as I have always been. It will give me great universal deal of value to understand myself awake and asleep.

Yes I do know, child. I know. Now, are you ready?
Yes I am, Parent. This is the grand moment, this it!

Good, very good you are doing, child. Hum ⋯ here we go.

The dreaming process

Now listen: whatever it is that you see, smell, taste, hear and feel now before you, you are dreaming it awake, and it is tuned by an adjusted tempered frequency. And whenever you fall asleep, in from whatever it is that you see, smell, hear and feel, you move through a connection of self-occupied space at a certain maximum speed, to a particular self-created desired dream as a particular self-created desired form of being, thus as such that you awake into whatever it is that you see, smell, hear and feel from sleep (in this very same moment), by tuning into its adjusted frequency.

Hum ⋯ you already know that I do not understand right, Parent?

Yes I know, child. This is what I am saying. For you to be able to experience any form or type of dream, you have to be awake in it.

Ah ⋯ okay, I see, Parent.

Good, child. Now while still awake in that dream, you experience it by tuned frequency of feeling, smelling, tasting, hearing or seeing it, or by using all the senses at once to have a full ultimate experience of that particular dream. Remember feeling?

Wow, okay ⋯ I think I am kind of getting you. I sort of understand what you are saying, now, Parent.

Good. Now whenever you sleep, in from that dream that you are in, you move through a connection that links you to any occupation you are, or may be at. When you move through that connection, you do it at a certain maximum speed to get to a particular dream as you imagine it by self-creating it according to your desires of thought. The speed that you move with, determines how quick you will reach a desired destination of a dream. Also you experience that moment of a dream that you have moved to, as any particular form or state of being as you imagine it by self-creating it according to your desires, which is in most cases, human, and scarcely ever foreign, animal, plant, water or any other matter or object—by seeing, hearing, smelling, tasting and feeling it by being awake in it and, as it.

Good, now I understand, Parent.
Good, and I am pleased, child.

I understood what you just said, Parent. Now tell me one thing here, you spoke of a connection that I move through, the one that links me to any occupation I may be, at any given time of moment. What is that connection, where is it, and why can I not see and touch it?

Thank you, child, I am glad you asked that question.
Why, Parent.

Because that connection, is the only thing that has been baffling you through your entire existence. It is the one that makes you scratch your head, and hold your chin with your fingers, while rolling your eyes in pondering wonder of thought. It is the one that makes you lose all answers that you have gathered, and places you on guessing possibilities. The sad great beautiful truth about it is that, you know what that connection is. You know it very well, as much as you know yourself, child. You have just not been willing to see and accept it as a link of connection.

I know it? Okay, what is it, Parent?
Space!

Space! Ah, come on! Really ··· space? Couldn't you come up with anything extraordinary, something that would amaze, amuse and wow me, Parent?

Well, this is the sad great beautiful truth, and it is that you know it, you know all of this and about it, child.

Okay, I see. But how am I connected to space, how does all of this work, what is really happening here, Parent? I still do not understand.

It is alright, I am here, child. Now listen, we are going to be more precisely practical about this, as to get you to a full understanding of it and, how it works, so participate with me.

Okay ⋯ I am ready.
Good, child.

Look around you, now, wherever it is, wherever you are, at this moment. Look at what you are holding now in your hands—or put and hold something. After ⋯ see a very near close-by suitable place where you would put whatever you are holding now, down on. Do you see it, and are still with me, child?

Yes, Parent.

Now, start to imagine and create yourself doing the following: See yourself putting it down (in your imagination) very ⋯ very ⋯ very slow down on that place. See and observe everything about yourself that your imagination creates, as you slowly think, when placing that which is in your hands, down. Do you see these thoughts as they unfold, child?

Yes I do, Parent.

Now then, literally and actually do what you have just imagined and saw doing, by putting down what you have in your hands, now, on that place. Do it at a pace that you normally spontaneously move at and do your everyday things, by following the exact manner at which you imagined placing it, child.

Okay, I see. What's this about though, Parent?

Good ⋯ and I will tell you, child.

I tell you this, it is to show, make you realize and be aware that you are connected to space. All space is already filled by the residuum-figment of your imagination that you create. As you were imagining putting what you have in hand down, slowly, you saw that you were filling or occupying a certain point in, or of space, and then move to another point of space from a point in space you are, and so on continuously move until you reached a desired place or point to put what you have in hand, down. After imagining it, you realized, and that is to say you made it a reality, by literally and actually moving through the essence of residuum-figment of your imagination as previously seen and thought, as a singular crystalized physical being. By this I mean that the essence is crystalized at a particular point of space that you occupy, to experience only that point of moment wholly.

Okay, wow that is, hum ⋯ well explained. But tell me, dearest Parent, why do I not see myself clearly, everywhere I am in space, now? I mean why is every point in space that I occupy not crystalized and clearly visible to sight? Why do I only see, experience and feel only one of me at one current point in moment, and not any other form or being, or many of other me? Please tell me, I mean it would really be helpful if I could see myself when I am over there or here. You see; I would be able to make judgment of my doings and rectify what needs to be, if I could.

Good, very good, child. You are just doing good and, asking the right questions. I know that the very question that you have asked is the one that you have struggled, searched and waited on, for its answer. And now that it is here, your curiosity awaits avidly in anticipation.

Yes I am, Parent. I have been confused and struggling to figure it out, and I just can't seem to work my wit around it.

153

I am here, child, and I will tell you why.

Now I tell you this, because it is the reason why you do not see what you have asked. This is what I say—it is because you choose not to. You choose not to see and physically crystalize every point of being that you are at in space, as to not make it real, and that is to say realize, by disregarding your thoughts as you see them, by ignoring.

Wow, okay, I choose not to? And why is that so, Parent?

Now listen, child, for what I am saying is your truth. And this is what I say: It is because deep down in the pumping heart of your consciousness you are aware of what is really happening here. Now, you are aware that, if you were to physically crystalize every point of being that you are at in space, then that means you would and will not be able to move, just as your conscious is certain, and realizes this (because you will be everywhere all over—, which indeed you already are, In the likeness of others!).

Okay ⋯ hold on ⋯ you just wait a minute here. What do you mean that I will not be able to move, and that I am everywhere, parent?

I mean that you will not be able to move, because you will have filled and crystalized every single point in and of space, that you have imagined and created yourself being at, child—and so far you have been pretty much everywhere in and by thought.

I still do not understand.

Oh well, it is okay. I will write a picture for you as so you may understand, and clearly see.

154

Now here is the written picture in truth, behold, and picture this: We are observing a picture of you within your bedroom. Your bedroom picture consists of physical crystalized remnants essence of you, for a week. Every turn and toss on your bed, and every step of walk round about in your bedroom, and every action of doing in any point of space that has occurred, and you have been, in a week, in your bedroom, is clustered and cluttered, stacked on each other, and it is clearly and perfectly seen on and in your bedroom canvas picture. This meaning that, everywhere you have been, you are physically visible and present at the same time, in all points, in this picture that we are imagining and creating.

Do you see this written picture, child ⋯ the imagery?
Yes I do, Parent.

Now, do you think you will be able to move to any point in that picture, child?

Nope, I do not see that because I am all over the place. I mean it is useless if I can't move, while I have moved to anywhere I am already, because of seeing myself being at a different particular point from where I am, experiencing it and, doing something different than I am now. And also by blocking and preventing myself by being in front and everywhere tightly closely around myself. Wow! And also this means that, I will be one solid pile of matter of myself altogether, going nowhere and being everywhere all at once. Wow ⋯ wait, and also again, this means that to the core of my conscious, like you said, Parent, I am aware and do realize that this is what is really happening. Actually I do realize this now. I know that I am not moving, thus only experiencing each part of myself separately uniquely wholly in its moment.

You got it, child. Yes indeed, why would you want and choose to do what you see yourself doing already? When you can just watch yourself from where you are, without moving, doing all that you are doing in this now moment.

Hum ⋯ okay, I see and I understand. Wow, so this is what you are saying—you are saying it is like filling my bedroom with a thousand people altogether at once, at different congested points, doing different things. Now because it will be so full and clustered, none will be able to move anywhere or do anything.

It is like a dozen-multiple of the same twins, child.
Ah, I see. I remember that.

Well then, you are correct, child. You do get now, you understand. You should be celebrating and wiggle that behind of yours. Stand up, smile and dance to your understanding. Rejoice and be happy, now, in this moment, child.

I may not be hopping and jumping as you would expect, but I am smiling, Parent. And I do understand.

Good, child.

Now that you understand that space is a connection that links you to any point you maybe, within itself. And also, now, at the deep rooted core of your consciousness; you now know and have realized that you are not moving, but just simply crystalizing a certain desired point for its sole experience; we can proceed further.

Yes, that is true. Now you spoke of an adjusted tempered frequency, Parent, what is that exactly, I mean what is it about?

Yes my good child. Be present here, now, in this moment. You have asked a question that shakes and intrigues the universe: the one that brings excitement to all creation, for you are asking and talking about it. It makes the universe dance, and make movement of joy that tickle, in celebration of reveling its truth. Songs and sounds of harmony pierce through the void to form creation. I tell you this, everything that you see now, here, and even the things you have absolutely consciously not crystalized in their particular points in space, as so you may not see them, is of a total existing subtle self-created frequency of vibration.

Vibration is caused by movement, without movement there is no vibration, and therefore no frequency to tune in to! Movement is caused by desire for and to a specific particular course. Without desire, there is no movement, and thus no creation of experience for what already exists as whole, for it is going nowhere, and doing nothing at all. When there is no desire, movement, vibration and frequency altogether, there is ultimately nothing in experience and, image.

Now, in order to create something of desires, that is to say to form creation into being, there is motion of movement towards it. This means that there is movement round-up, down-about, to and at any point—to whatever it is that you are going to, to create. This movement creates vibration, and then forms and leaves waves of frequency at a particular specific point as a residuum.

Now, with all the points of frequency connected, an image or a drawing of the desired full outcome is created and thus seen by being crystalized as a whole. It is a drawing because you are drawn and attracted towards it. You are drawn to something, because you are attracted to it. You are attracted to something because you desire it, from the image that you see. Desire creates the drawn attraction to exist, in your space! Remember that I said you are singular being with two polarities, and moving between them on equilibrium within yourself. And also, a being as you already are, consists of only creation, and creation consists of only a polarity that repels itself to a different flow of movement and form to create itself as duality and or even multiples.

Oh my word. This all makes sense and it is starting to add up now, I mean I understand what you are saying, Parent.

Good, very good, child.

Now that you are getting clearer on this, we are proceeding, child. Now, listen again. Be with the words, put all attentive emotions to what follows, because this is what you have desired to know, thus you have drawn its attraction towards you. This is what I say; I tell you this, every time, and each of every single moment you choose and fully decide to lay your body to rest and fall asleep, this is what happens:

Every time whenever you sleep, your body becomes and breaks numbly-partially-lightly, and or totally loose from its current crystalized form of being in vibration. It vibrates in a tinkling, softly-lightly sharp and very quick-sonic movement, and leaves the residuum of your figments, at that current point in space—

May you please explain, right there, what you mean by that, Parent.

Okay listen to this then. Every time when you sleep, your body becomes numbly-partially-light. It is numbly partial because, you can still feel the irritation of a fly on your body when you are sleeping, and even feel the good sensation of someone slightly running a finger on your body. This ability of breaking apart is possible through stillness and calm of the body. When still, the vibrating figment of essence does not focus, hold and retain one body in space of all the other ones. Thus it can break loose from it to any other ones in space.

Okay, I got that, Parent.

Good. Now also, and or, it becomes totally numb because sometimes you fully and totally break loose from the current crystalized body in essence, thus as such you do not feel that fly, or someone running a finger, whether you are under the influence of alcohol and or any drug, or not.

Okay good, I got that one as well, Parent, thanks!

It is a sure thing with me, child. Now, when it breaks, whether partially or totally, it vibrates (meaning that it moves) in a subtle tinkling sensational, softly-lightly-sharp, and very quick-sonic movement. You always feel this slight vibration, whether conscious or not. You can even feel it now if you want, child.

Okay ⋯ I got that, now I understand, Parent.
Good.

So now then, when you sleep, your atomic and microscopic body cells move and vibrate very quickly or fast. In order to find, or to be in or at a certain place as a particular form of the same or different, you adapt and adopt, that is to say that—(you adjust to its frequency to be as it is). Once you have adjusted to a certain frequency, you become it, thus as such that you experience the drawn attracted desire of creation that you have moved towards into.

Now, when you partially break from your current body, you thus definitely as well equally partially break into, feel and experience some residue or residuum of your beings, at some points, by moving adjustably and tuning through to them. This means that you partially feel what you are being and doing when in your dream, and partially feel and are aware of yourself, when you are sleeping. This is why you can still hear sounds of people and things, and even feel when being touched, while still hearing and feeling your presence in your dream. You partially experience and feel both realized sides of truths about yourself, and thus return to where you desire the most, for a suitable desired experience for some durable moment. Hence thus as such you do not remember where you were particularly in your dream because you spend nanoseconds experiencing moments of multiple ripples of realities, instead of holding account for one unified moment by maintaining thoughts.

Now then, also when you totally break from your current body, you thus definitely as well equally totally break into, feel and experience residuum of your being, at any point, by moving adjustably and tuning through to them. This means that you totally feel what you are being and doing when you are dreaming, it becomes a wholly experience of your dream. This is why you will and would not even hear a single sound of a person, a pin drop, or things in your surrounding environment of the place you are and remember sleeping at, and do not even feel when being touched. This happens because you are ultimately experiencing a single creation that you have adjusted and tuned into by its frequency—totally wholesome. Hence thus as such you remember your dreams of where you were being and doing, because you only experienced it—uniformly and hold account of that moment, just as your reality now, and nothing else but that.

Now, child, this is exactly what I meant, when I said that, 'whatever it is that you see, smell, taste, hear and feel now before you, you are dreaming it awake, and it is tuned by an adjusted tempered frequency.'

Wow ··· I love this part, of talking about dreams. I mean I do get it, everything is becoming clearer and easy. Thanks, Parent!

It's a Pleasure my good friendly child.

Now I have another question for you.
Of course you do, child.

Ah! Anyways ··· why when I move and dream being in a different place and creation, does the person next to me or around, still sees me? I mean do I not disappear, since I do move to somewhere else, Parent?

Good question, child. Now let me see ⋯ I know have the answer to that lying somewhere around here! What's in this file? Oh ⋯ nothing ⋯ come on ⋯ come on ⋯ come on ⋯ Hum, It has got to be here somewhere!

Really, Parent? Come on ⋯ there is no time for that now. Jokes aside please!

Hey, I was just trying to cool things down in here. It was getting too hot and intense, child.

Okay cool, I assume you suggest that I have and take another sip of a drink and or snack on something, or I should just go take a shower and then go see some friends for a while?

Whatever rocks your boat, child. At least you are smiling again.
Okay, cool. Can we get back to serious stuff that matter now!

Sure. Now, to answer your question, remember that you are everywhere, and that is to say at every and any point in space, you are. For you to still be visible and for someone to see you, is because that, that person is in their own experienced crystalized reality of you sleeping, at that point, where they are, in that moment. In order for that person not to see and experience your presence, in one way—he or she would have to physically leave from where you are, just as you have done, by sleeping, which then they will be moving from where you are, as so not to see you, in their own other different dream (of where you are not). And also he or she can move by simply walking away to a farther distanced place that is out of range and sight from where you are. By them walking and moving away, you are thus not in their reality, and yet you still exists, in the same space.

Now also, the person can just simply fall asleep right next to where you are, and totally break into his or her own desired reality, of a separated dream from yours. Since you will both be in different places of reality ultimately and

161

totally, you both each equally do not exist respectively, in the presence of each other's reality of dreams, and to where you are sleeping, now, in this moment. You will both be next to each other, and yet, not feel each other's presence, because you are totally somewhere other than where you are both sleeping. You will be next to each other, and yet still, be in different places of desired drawn attracted creation—that you go to by free will, to see its image and experience it.

The same is said for when leaving the body partially. When you both leave the body partially, you both experience each other partially next to each other and your surroundings, while still respectively experiencing and feeling your dream reality of where you have adjusted and tuned into by a frequency, partially. So now, the person who sees you, chooses, and desires to have, feel and see you, by choice, of loving to, in their reality, child.

Mm, I see, Parent.
Good, very good you are, still.

How to dream

Remember, child, that 'whatever it is that you see, smell, taste, hear and feel, now before you, you are dreaming it awake, and it is tuned by an adjusted tempered frequency. And whenever you fall asleep, in from whatever it is that you see, smell, hear and feel, you move through a connection of self-occupied space at a certain maximum speed, to a particular self-created desired dream as a particular self-created desired form of being, thus as such that you awake into whatever it is that you see, smell, hear and feel from sleep, by tuning into its adjusted frequency.'

Now, again I require your presence. Be here in creation as creation itself and as a creator of dreams, for I am telling you how to willingly and consciously dream. I am giving you already known and existing factual empirical objective secrets of how to realize and create your desires in and of a dream. These are the forever kept in plain sight secrets, of how to enter dreams, now in your world, of your own dream.

Okay, that's just awesome. You mean after this, I will be able to control and dream at my own will, Parent?

Well yes, yet all depending on your will; being able to control and allowing yourself to enter different states and dimensions, consciously, child. And I will tell all about what you should choose to do, and what not to choose to do, (only by your own highest choice of course), and some hazards of danger.

Okay. Wow, jeez, you mean that there are some hazards and cautions I have to take count to, and I have a choice of following or not, Parent?

Yes indeed you do, just as always, child.
Okay I am ready. Please, may we begin!

Now this is how you do it, as you already have done it and are doing it now, child. Whenever you sleep at any moment, especially night, you lie down in a horizontal flat position facing up, just as you would stand straight. This position is ideal and particularly advantageous because your body weight does not rest on any part of itself, thus creates flexibility and mobility. Retaining and control of any muscle and parts should be let loose. This means that your hands, arms, legs, neck, fingers and toes, jaws and, specifically especially your genital organ muscle should not feel or be stiff or contracted. Hands beside, and shoulders relaxed.

Once having settled and comfortable, you will feel the weight of your body under your back on the surface you are lying and resting on—or sleeping on. At this point, no movement of any sort by an inch should occur, and should be

163

in a very still restful state. The only movement that should take place is your stomach and chest, from the easy subtle diligent flow of breathing. This still position means that you let go and lose all willing control of the body by relaxing. Be still and allow your weight to become one with what you are sleeping on. In a moment of time (at any rate), you will feel the same mass, as one, all over around, and your body weight will not be independent because it will be one with what you are sleeping, or resting your body on.

Wow ⋯ that sounds like a lot of work, Parent.

Nah ⋯ not really so, child, all you have to do is to sleep lying facing up loosely relaxed and still. I was just verbose and at the same time concise. I just wanted you to know and understand ⋯ you know? Kind o' drilling it in!

Ah ⋯ I should have known, there we go again. Can we please ⋯ get back on track, and focus!

Oh yes of course my sweet child.

Now, once your weight is one with what you are resting on and having lost all willing control of muscles of the body, you will feel light. Child—, brace yourself because this is where it gets interesting.

Ah please, can you just say it already. You are suspending me here, and its killing me, Parent.

Well ⋯ how about I leave you hanging there, for a while? Okay I' m kidding, I will be serious now. Jeez I' m sure you are thinking that this is all getting hoary now, child.

Yes, actually I do. You should see my face right now.

Oh I do see it, child. The way you roll your eyes taking a sigh and, shaking your head thinking that I am being ridiculous ⋯ and then laughing because this is all crazy ⋯ yah I can definitely see you.

Now, once you start feeling light—you then feel the slight tinkling sensational-vibration of your body cells moving. This is the process advancing to you being more aware and conscious of self. At this point, the vibration seeks to center itself. Your sexual gland becomes active and produces a reproductive fluid that discharges without any external impetus activity, and gives an internal orgasm. The flow of vibration tinkles and moves (gently charged)—smooth through your gland towards your navel. At this point in this great moment, your navel and chest slightly and smoothly contract inwards (you will feel hollow inside around your belly). This is the moment your body starts to break loose from itself in vibration of light essence.

Depending on the targeted and tuned frequency (your dream desire of experience), you experience moving at a particular speed towards that frequency you are attracted to. The experience is felt as if falling down in an abyss (just like in a rabbit hole) ⋯ it so because of speed. Speed, whether in vertical or horizontal motion creates the impression of falling. That is why when in or on a vehicle of over a speed of, say, maybe 300 km/h, you would feel as if falling, even though travelling horizontally across. Now then, the slower the speed, the bumpier and gripping it gets to the destination of the desired frequency because (you are not jumping some occurring events all at once), thus you feel bumping on them, yet but rather experience the reality of where you are slowing down at.

The faster and quicker the speed (super-sonic), the more instantaneous the desired destination of frequency in vibration is produced. Past beyond that, you will feel floating about, and extremely light, yet in a fixed position. You will be able to walk, or fly or (appear in transformation) in any place as anything immediately. The returning trip back is easy and quick because you

165

fall back where you came from—which is on yourself. And again, the experience is the same as going, it all depends on the speed you use. Now then, since you will be conscious and aware of your visited self-created reality in your dream, you will know of its existence and it will thus remain as a memory and can as it will, be visited again just by thinking and remembering it. Yet all this depends on your desired creativity and will, of all of this.

Wow ⋯ oh, okay. So that's it, it's that simple and easy. That's all I have to do if and when I want to dream consciously?

No, that is not all. There are different ways of doing it, and you have done them all, you are just not conscious about it. What I have explained, is what takes place every time you sleep. It matters not how you sleep. You can and may as you have, sleep sitting up, standing drunk against a wall or something, or in any position you can possibly think of on your bed, child. I am only making you aware of it. And know this again, that this is not a must practice or do. It depends on you and how much avid you are to realize this and, advantageously take use of its powerful creativity to have your desires, fantasies, imagination, needs and wants met immediately in all aspects of the universal dream that you are in now to experience the power that you have.

Just by a snap of a finger, and a tick of a second, you can and will have it. It is easy to do this, yes, yet it takes some great efforts and time into it and a willing spirit. You can as you may by will, even have it done within a day, just as you do ⋯ if not, or even a year, or more than that. It is just like learning how to walk, or talk for that matter. And once you have completely understood it, and are able to manipulate it, you will be able to do it in any position or form, and awake all the time without having to sleep at all. You will see what great power you have within. For once it is willed and controlled, life is a fantastic magical blissful creativity. You will see that you have everything, by creating it now, as you see it. And it will just appear as you know it.

Well ⋯ oh wow. That sounds very good, Parent. I can' t wait to get to that stage. So is that all, or is there more to this?

There is more, child.

Okay, I am good and set for more. Give it to me baby, just the way I like it. You just keep it coming and I will take. Why? Because I can!

Ah ⋯ just listen to you, child.

Oh well, you can' t blame me can you? The stuff that you give to me and the way you go about it, is good. And I don' t know how you do it, but it sure is damn good!

Now listen, be current and present, in this beautiful moment. I am helping and giving you the tips and tricks on how not to endanger and terrifyingly horrify yourself, in your own loving creation of a dream that you tune yourself into—as you venture.

Danger and horror! Wow, that sounds scary, Parent. I am feeling dreadful already.

Yes, danger, you have been in one before, and you are always nervous, scared and sweaty whenever you encounter such situations, and you never seem to know what to do, but always run away or freeze and remain paralyzed in fear of loud internal screams that you stammer and murmur in your sleep and dream (both at same time). Sometimes you do not even understand the experience you have chosen.

Are you talking about sleep paralysis, Parent?

Well something like of that nature, yet on a larger scope of understanding.

Okay ⋯ tell me all about it, Parent.

Now, listen again, for this is what happens, and this is how you can by will, avoid or prevent it. Now, for the very reason that there are many realities that you have created from your own thoughts through your entire life out, you are thus assured to re-experience them as you encounter by going through them in being; while you think, at any time again. Well, like we have said before many times, this simply means that your thoughts are real and can be relived. With this truth being had and held in mind; you have had and you still do at some times, have thoughts such as being attacked by someone or a thing—and in your superficial superstitions and religious sense of it, you are attacked by a great dark creature or a group of demons that intend to destruct your reality, from that thought in your dream, and it also happens that you even have forced sex with them, sometimes. You have dreamt a snake crawling and creeping under your body on your bed. You dream fighting, flying, having riches ⋯ and the list just goes on ⋯ and on.

All of these dreams were and are still experienced because you created them from thought of choice by simply imagining from any time of the day in any moment. You create them in this manner that follows: It all starts with a simple conversation with someone, and by you saying "just imagine ⋯" being happy, attacked, raped, shot, rich, and or poor and so on. Justly by saying and imagining these, you then create what you see from your thoughts constructively, and then put into words, to give the other an understanding.

Mm ⋯ I remember this part, Parent. You told me how my imagination works to create.

Good, very good then.

Now, with the confronted faced reality of truth of an entire ocean of your thoughts everywhere from imagination in your life. Whenever you choose to enter a dream consciously, you should mind and deeply consider what you are thinking, in the moment, from your imagination. Because, when you enter a dream, you go through a single moment of a thought, of various events, and this is to say that you go through old and new thoughts, of which some you have forgotten because they are of a great deal long ago when you thought about them now. Therefore choose to channel your thoughts away from bad things that you think now, or have thought before. When in the process of dreaming consciously and venturing into different dimensional states and, you think of a bad thing, you will be drawn to it. The experience will be felt wholly, totally and completely consciously as what you consider your life of reality right now. Now, because the dimension that you will be in, will be real, as in realized, everything will and becomes clear and not blur. You will be able to distinguish, label and recognize your dream environment for what it is.

Now, coming to monitoring your thoughts, this is what I say: Be careful not to enter a bad dream from thought. Because when you do, it frightens and leaves you in tumultuous state, which of course, frustrates you desperately to escape from your situation by running, in fear, or by instantly appearing at a different place in that same dimension of that dream. By doing this, (in fear and confusion), you then prolong the stay and spend a great time thinking about and of running away from what is coming to you, in that same dream that you are conscious of, instead of thinking what is not.

Now, because of fear and confusion of panic, you then willingly lose the ability and control of your conscious dream. When this happens, you allow your thoughts, which are everywhere and anything as you have thought, to control your experiences, by you not choosing consciously or being aware of what you walk or step into. By doing this, you then again, go into and move through dimensions of your previous thought by not your own influence yet of your own creation and cause of choice. You will experience things happening to you without knowing why, and you will be in places not knowing where and how. The experience becomes a frightening, tormenting confusing and an unpleasant reality. In the occurrence and events of this horrifying experience, your body that you left sleeping, in one great memorable earthly event, is witnessing and thus reacts in shock and terror as it shivers to these events and moments, for it does not believe, and indeed, it really does not believe it (that it just went there⋯ Gosh!).

Wow, okay just slow it down Parent. I just need to think about this. So this is what happens?

Yes, yet wait because I am still saying, child: Your witnessing and sleeping body transmits sounds by voice of words by calling and crying out help to try to escape and break free the connection from the other dimension of a dream it is consciously in. Yet it is very difficult for it to leave because it is in a total realization of where it is in that dimension, thus it thinks it is real and cannot go anywhere because that's the only reality, and does not know how it got there, by forgetting the way back and that also it is still alive (somewhere sleeping) yet only witnessing the experience of its adventures from thoughts.

Wow that is just deep. Ah, ah ⋯ mm ⋯ no ways, it's just too much. Yet I must say that it sounds like dreams I have had before, Parent.

Yes child, it is so. You have experienced being trapped in your dream before, (and you still are now—but awake in it), and you cry help in hope that someone may shake you off from it, and have struggled on your own, to come back to your own loving reality so that you do not remain long in that dream, if you do not do it yourself. Yet here is the caution: When you forget and do not remember how to come back, your body that you have known and spent time with, through your life as you remember, will be partially affected by the events that occur in that other dimension you are in. The longer the stay, the longer afflictions to your life now in this state, of that bad dream of any sort from your thoughts.

Okay, and how is that, good Parent?

Now, listen for what I say next.

This is what happens: When travelling and experiencing different reality dimensions of a dream from where you are right now, and you get caught and entangled up in it by either its fantasy or horror. It will affect your current realm. Now, beginning from your horrific bad thoughts: Should it so happen that you engage and encounter any horrific thought from your imagination, you will experience it. When this happens (due to the fact that you realize it by seeing it), you will then present your experiences from that realm by reacting to them in this world, even though they are not here, in this world, yet are happening and real.

If and when you are up against monsters, and you scream and struggle in fear, shiver and cover yourself or try to fight back. That is exactly what will happen in this world (with your current body), in reaction through the solidarity of the link and connection of space. With that having being said, people of this world will tend to find your behavior very strange, and as most widely believed, abnormal (crazy). This is so because, they will not and they still do not see your experiences because you are creating them and experiencing away from where they are. Now because they will not understand, and thus have no tangible solution as to what is really going on with you, they will take you to a mental institution and give you all sorts of disease names. You will be labeled sick, unfit, crazy, stupid and or a danger to society and even yourself because of your violent and frightening reaction that you are experiencing in a different reality, that you output in to this world.

Your world will do this to you, as it is already, because it does not understand. And so it is as it should be that you will have created two conditions for yourself. First; you will be trapped in a different dimension. Second; you will be kept and trapped in a mentally ill institution. In a sense, it is more very

171

much likely as you would say, that you are experiencing a hell of a nightmare, yet in this case, in two dimensions of which you are conscious of, and cannot escape until you can, by will. And this is all on your choices, made of curious desires (when you think of how it would be if you were this or that and doing and being that or this!).

Wow, is that what really happens? I mean I have seen people who are crazy on the streets, so is that what really happens to them, and to the ones that are kept away as well or institutionalized, Parent? Is it because they see things we don' t?

Yes. I have told you before oh great good child on NOTHING that, no one is crazy yet only experiencing their dreams. And this is why I had told you that when you see a vagrant on the street, you should not judge, for you do not completely and fully know what they are up to—yet now it is that you know.

Mm ⋯ yes you did. Well wow, I don' t want to venture in to this conscious dreaming thingy if that' s how it is. I mean I could end up being crazy! Nope, it is just not my thingy at this moment.

Well this is what happens when you have a nightmare, and it can be controlled and willed, yet you only experience it for a good two minutes if not more than that. You are already doing it now in your life, yet you do not realize it and that it is, this is to say that you dreaming right now, remember?

Yes I do.

 And like I have said, oh good one, these you have experienced before and are still, yet only forgotten them. I am reminding and making you aware of it.

Wow, oh, okay.

Now listen, again, secondly: not only do you react to bad dreams, but also to good fantastic magical ones. Should it happen that you find yourself in blissful wonderful dream, you will also react to it when the connection is still linked. And remember that the longer the stay, the longer the experience is as well. So when and if caught up in your dream, and you are flying, jumping, or in an aesthetic world of fantasy and catching on awesomeness, you will experience in reaction to it. Your reaction will be gesticulated through waving, smiling and laughing, and giving out gestures to nothing of this realm of reality of a dream. And because the experience is not here, the world will find you abnormal.

Now listen to this, for it is what happens as you already are doing it. Choose to take good conscious cautions not to enter multiple dimensional states at same moment of time when dreaming, whether sleep lying on something, or consciously in movement as you have mastered.

Okay, what do you mean by that, oh good Parent?

Here is the danger to it: You should choose to experience one dimension of a dream wholly. This is to say that, always be in the moment of now, of this dream that you love. Because when in multiple dimension, you have to see to it, that each reality that is experienced, corresponds and relates well carefully in adjustment to its surrounding, while moving and being them at once. This means that you will control and manipulate yourself by attracting and leading yourself to each desire in any moment of all the dimensions you are in concomitantly. Now, should you lose focus of any of your beings, especially in a critical crucial moment, by shifting your attention completely to another one or more states of beings, you will thus distract its moment and purpose of its doing in that dimension.

Therefore this means that, whatever state of being and dimension you lose focus of in a crucial moment, will be affected by what is occurring in it

173

momentously, without you being aware because you are not focused to it. And by the time you realize by concentrating to it again—zoning back—you then find that you are experiencing something, or are at a brink of it. Whether falling, or run over by a car, knocking into something, or being struck by a meteorite or any of your familiar objects. With this reality having occurred, you will then blame the universe, and say that it is of great power and will beyond you, why that of such nature has happened. You choose to hold no responsibility and account of your own creation and ignorance in distraction. You rather say it is something you do not see by conventional names such as deity, the great one, omnipotent being, spirit, ancestors and even unknown gods. You do this as not to be blamed for your own actions.

Wow, so that's how it is? Really, is that how it is? I am just totally staggered by this truth. Wow!

Yes my good child, this is what happens and some of it you still do as you have done it. Is it not surprising, and ironically strangely funny that there is a moment in time whereby you were almost hit or knocked by a car, because you were not aware of it on its approach, only because you were thinking and focusing on something else beyond that moment you were currently in? I tell you this, it is exactly what happens. It is so because you are in multiple dimensions simultaneously. Instead of focusing and being in only one moment of now, you thus then create distanced thoughts in experience of them, now, at the same time. This is why when crossing the road and you think of something else (that distracts you in that moment); you see it and are not aware of what is happening around you now in this or that very same moment. By the time you snap back to this reality, you then realize ··· oops, I am here actually, I need to move—out of the way, quick!

Mm, you are getting all the way through to me, good Parent. I mean, I am actually realizing this now. Well I suppose I should say thank you. Thank you!

You are all welcome good, child.

Now, not only do you experience multiple dimensions and realities in crucial moments, yet also, in almost everything you do every day. You do this from a vantage point, in retrospect, by being nostalgic or by reminiscing and cogitating while still doing something, by seeing another thing in space, from thought in the same spot of space you are in. You would be cooking and dealing with hot stove or fire, and you just zone out by thinking of the past or creating the future by thought. Again, by the time you zone back, your finger or hand is burning or is on a hot surface. You would even bump on to a pole or someone on the streets because you are partially here in this reality.

There are many simple things that you call errors that you do, because of sleep living or walking. You sleep here, and awake there, in a different dimension of thought in your dream of desire—in one and same space and time.

Wow, okay, sleep walking, is that what is meant by that?
Yes good child, that is what is meant.

Okay, I hear you. I got it, Parent. I must say that this is all making sense now. I mean you were right when you said that I am everywhere in space, and that I do not choose to see myself all over everywhere. I mean really, think about it! Because to control all states of being in all dimensions, I would be here and, would just be a puppeteer to my realities by instruction of thought in my dream! Wow, that is just amazing. How did you know all of this, good Parent? I do not mean to question your intelligence here, yet I would love to know.

I am simply justly aware of it in realization from your experiences that are happening now, of which are mine, child.

Okay, fair enough.

Good, very good.

I have listened and I am grateful for the true realization. So far you have told me how to enter a dream by sleeping, and how I do it almost every day in thought of imagination by not being aware of it. Yet I have not come to understand, or you have not made it clear of how I can be anything instantly now, or how I can be rich, just to be specific, Parent.

Mm ··· oh child, you and money though.

What? I can't help it being tempted to use this opportunity, advantageously as you have said, for my own "selfish" needs.

Well the answer to this question is simple, and I have told you of it already, yet you are not aware that it is the answer. Yet I will make it clear for you, though you will not like the answer.

Okay, that's just a downer already. I already feel that I won't like it, but I am very much interested of what you will say, Parent.

It's not much of what you expect, but here we go. Now, for you to experience anything instantly now, "just to be specific", "riches" —

Ha, ha, ha ··· very funny.

Listen, child. Just like I have said, you would have to sleep and enter that dimension you see yourself in, as being whatever you are, or rich. By this, I mean that you would have to leave this dimension, and go to the other one, to experience it wholly and completely. Yet for this, you are not ready child.

Can you please be clearer on this and elaborate, Parent.

You would have to leave your current body or, just disappear into another singular realm, as so not to experience partial multiple dimensions. You give yourself only one reality of experience from the image that you see, which in this case of your question is riches and wealth. Remember that multiple dimensions or thoughts, affect each other. You will experience lack here, and yet still know that you are rich, in experience of it from somewhere else. Therefore thus this current method of yours does not create instant results, because you are not ready to leave here, now.

Meaning what exactly?
That you do not want to die or disappear from here yet, child!

Well of course yes, I am not ready for that.
That is what I said.

Mm ⋯ so let me get this straight and right. I am everywhere I think I am. I experience myself only being here because I do not want to experience multiple dimensions. I visit some realities of my dream unconsciously and sometimes consciously either when I am asleep or awake. I could be anywhere now as I am, yet I am not ready to leave because I love it here where I am. How was that?

Good, very good. Now you are getting to understand yourself. I am happy for you, child.

Thanks.

Now listen oh good one. Once having understood and have mastered how to dream consciously alert by going to any dimension at any moment, perception of time ceases its flow from how you currently know it. You will be able to keep tabs of events—, yet in a unified moment as a wholly singular unified being. The term tomorrow or yesterday, will stop to exist from thoughts and lips because, you will render-tend doing things now as you think in the moment.

Now being the master of your dream, with whatever you think from imagination, you will thus go or venture in to it instantly as you now think. This is to say that, whenever you think and should it happen that you imagine being where your mother or father is at, you then thus instantly appear there. This happens because you are now clear, and this means that you see your imagination clearly, the creation is purely crystal clear as you know it (just as clear as you know this reality). You will think to be here, and you will be here. You will think to be there, and you will be there. You will think you are this, and be this. You also will think you are that, and you will be that! Everything will be exactly as you think, from all the possible options of imagination instantly as you see it, that are in your memory, good child.

Wow, you just got me all excited there. You mean then after, I will be anything of everything! You mean I could even go to my ex and have sex just for fun, and create it the way I want it? Oh ⋯ oh wait ⋯ even better, I could be with that fantasy dream beautiful lover of mine, and just be happy and make love all the time. I can even take a trip to the moon and back, just like that. Wow, it actually sounds like I am a superman-woman. Goku strength, here I am representing all humanity and all nations of species in the universe, great!

Mm ⋯ well fortunately that is exactly how it is. Yet this is the kind of excitement I cautioned you of; for the exact reason, you will think and create being at or on the moon, and thus appear to be there without even knowing the conditions of your external atmosphere in space because of not completely knowing or understanding your true power (and have forgotten how it is there), and thus solidify and freeze in space. Being in the deep ocean blue without even knowing what is there. Changing forms justly for the experience—going in and out. You will be moving quickly through time and space, doing all that you want and wish (just as you are now) by your will yet without any purpose or considerations of your doings and actions. Causing distraction and destruction to things and life itself, thus disturbing the universal dream as whole in experience of your just causes, will and power. And with all of this contemplated in mind, it is as such that you will self-destruct as many times without even having fear of the outcome, because you will now know that you cannot and will not ever die and that all will be okay, because you will have consciously felt, seen, heard and experienced it many a time by the cause of your wild adventures in the imagination of a dream. You will not fear death, yet rather thus bring death to it—((**fear**) that which you fear and do not like). And it is as such that at this moment, you realize that you have done nothing at all productive with your life in experience of it now in this moment.

Mm, okay ⋯ I see, Parent.

This is why I firmly stated and cautioned you about your thoughts. It is so not to endanger, horrify or terrify oneself in self-destruction. Again, good child, look to your thoughts of what you think, for you are thus creating by choice.

Cool, I got it. Thanks!

Now then, moving back to time as you know it: Once you have mastered your dream and how to dream—, not only can you experience it as a singular being, yet and or also as multiple states of being as we have said. This means you would, can, as you will as are now, exhaust one being at a particular certain dimension, and leave it to rest on the bed, or at any point in any occurring event, to later pursue its purpose when you come back to it. With this beard in mind, for you and to you only, time will be tampered and will not exist as you know it. It is so because you will consciously realize you have safely secured one body of many others on a bed sleeping, yet also precisely very conscious that you are somewhere else as or in a different body in the

179

same or different dimension, experiencing your meanwhile desires as you wish. By this time it will be very apparent, (as it is not now), that there is only one time. You will be sleeping for a good six hours on this side, yet having the greatest time of your life, in another dimension or the same—at the same time. There will be no difference between day and night, for such a thing will not exist because you are as you will be awake all the time in realizing, and are conscious of what is really going on here!

Mm ⋯ yes, I do remember that you told me about this on NOTHING, Parent.

Well, yes good child. I did make a promise to you that I will explain how dreams are and work. And also how to be that which you wish to be in your dream, now.

Yes, I also remember that as well. Thank you. So is there more or that's just it on how to dream, Parent?

And that is it, my fair good one.
Well it has been good, Parent.

And it has only been my pleasure, child.

Reality of dreams

Now listen, child. A dream is real and alive. It so because you awake it by being awake in it, thus you are alive in and with what you realize. Everything and anything exist within a whole universal dream in knowledge, and is, just as it can be, experienced fractionally. A reality of a dream is experienced by fully desired ranged sight of the whole entire existence.

I don't—

It is okay, child, I know. I am explaining. Now this is what I mean. Just like we said before that, you know everything and that you are wise, yet rather just only forgetting to remember knowing. This means that in reality everything exists, both the seen and unseen, in knowledge of it.

I hear you, Parent and you told me about this, but I am still not getting what you are trying to saying.

Okay this is what I am saying: Everything that you see, now, is a small experienced fraction of an entire dream of your knowledge. I mean that you experience only what you see, and what you see, is what you totally desire, and what you desire you attract by moving towards it in drawing. And whatever it is that you see, is only of a range of your eyes can reach by sight.

This is to say that, when in a house, you only see and experience things that are in the house because that is what you only see, and yet you know very well what lies outside and beyond your house. And when outside your house, you only see and experience things that are outside your house, because that is what you only see, observe and experience, and yet still you know very well what is in your house (and what happens in it). When in a certain city, you experience and see things that are within that city, yet you do not see and experience what is in the other city, yet you still know that, that city exists whether you see it or not. When in this country, you see and experience things that are in this country, yet you do not see and experience what is in the other country, yet you still know that, that other country exists whether you see it or not. When on this planet; you see and experience what is on this planet, yet you do not see and experience what is on another planet, and yet you still know that it exists whether you see it or not.

The same is said for milky-ways and galaxies ⋯ so on and on; you are in this one now, and yet you do not experience the other, but you know that it exists.

It so because it is a whole entire big dream of your creativity, and you only experience the most closely favorable and desired fraction of the whole universal dream! You only experience a small fraction, yet it is within your knowledge that everything exists (on the choice of experiencing it), both the seen and unseen, child! You know everything, child, because it is within your dream, that you have created everything. Your dream and no one else's dream but yours!

Wow ⋯ okay ⋯ I think I got that. I guess that was the only way you could make me understand hey?

No ⋯ you just only chose to understand the second explanation over the first, and yet what I have said is ambiguous.

Okay good, I got it, thanks, Parent.
It's a pleasure.

Now then, since a dream is so big, so broad and universal, and everything exists and is real in it. Therefore this means that everything is real in creation of it, and because you see it by desiring it, in your love. It is real because you are drawn to it, and you are here because you love it, and what you love, now, in this experienced moment, is only a small fraction of all creation by you, and you thus see your creation. Only certain desired and favorable parts of your creation are experienced. Therefore this means that, right now, you are awake in your dream, because you see what you are dreaming. And you are where you are right now, because you love it and have made a choice of it. Now, therefore, should you think that you are happy, sad, struggling and or suffering in agony in this dream that you love so much, you should be aware that you keep on coming back by waking up every single morning to it, and it being so, you leave your beloved bodies right were you think and, have caused yourself to know that you are happy, sad, struggling and or suffering in agony and hate the condition of where it is.

Yes, I have come to understand that, now, Parent. I understand how dreams are now.

Good, now listen, yes indeed, dreams are very, very real. Therefore whatever it is that you experience, you should know that it is real, and you are the cause creator for that exact experienced moment, yet you can change it and manipulate it to your own desires.

I now know, Parent.
Good.

Now then, this is what happens in reality of your now dream. Whenever you vibrate and tune into another dimension of your dream as a certain frequency, partially or totally by waking into it, you become present in that moment, and you appear as you are, this is to say partially or totally, whether in the same or different dimension. Now, should you appear and present yourself partially dense in any dimensional state of a dream, those to whom and what you show and reveal yourself to, will experience you vaguely translucent in your opalescent state, luminously. Now, because you will be physically in a vague translucent state, your appearance will be holographic as projected by thoughts, and you will be considered not real because your physic will appear in a partial resemblance.

This happens because the amount of movement used to create a vibration that tunes to a frequency is weak (blurry thoughts), thus you appear partial. When you are in this state, in any dimension: communication, contact and touch becomes difficult as compared to being totally whole (in a dense crystalized physical thought). This is to say that words that use vibration from your voice are not uttered clearly, if so nothing at all because of partiality. And contact or touch of different totally complete tuned vibration of physical objects or matter becomes a struggle. Your weight of dense matter is less, hence you become light and are able to move and fly around and move swiftly to destinations in essence. And also the tuned vibration of partiality is spread and semi-centered, this is to say that you radiate subtle rays of light and appear to be glowing luminous, thus the very reason it is felt and can be seen and felt from some distance by other physical beings of object of matter because of the faint vibrations and waves of light, in rays or sound.

Now, when in you are in this vague partial light translucent luminous state, any equivalent or greater external light source, blends and overpowers your current frequency, which in turn makes you more less visible to be distinguishable as anything particular because you will have become one with that source. So far, the most effective external greater overpowering light source that you are close to and are familiar of in your dream is the sun. This is why you appear invisible whenever and when you are in a vague partial light translucent state during day time. For you to be able to establish communication and contact during day time (in this partial state), you would have to choose to concentrate your frequency of vibration to a total state of being (physical appearance) and not partial. Also communication and contact to or with any object or being can as it is already, be established during the period you call night time when in a partial state because there is no light of sun that overpowers you with it shadow of light.

Hum ⋯ I hear what you are saying, and I just let you go on there. I don' t quite understand, but from what I have picked you are talking about me being in partial state in any dimension of a dream. Basically when I am in partial state, I struggle to touch and hold things, and even to utter words. During the day I am not clearly visible, if at all not seen, because I am sort of transparent and translucent, and because I am overpowered by light source that is greater, which is the sun. I can mostly be seen—when in a partial state— during night time because there is no sun, and that it is dark, yet still not tangibly visible because of partiality, and I also it being so I radiate subtle light that makes me appear glowing or luminous. And also, "with this great truth", as you would put it, to those I appear and present myself to, will consider me not to be real, because of the condition of state I am in. How's about that, am I right?

Yes you are, child. You got it.
Okay, good. But now tell me, what does this mean though, Parent?

Yes, this is what it means. Now that you are clear on this matter, listen for this is what I say: Knowing that whenever you present yourself in a partial state, you are not physically tangible, and you are considered not real to and by those who perceive or see you. Know this, whenever someone or something visits or encounters you, and it or they appear partially luminous translucently in your reality, you tend to perceive the encounter and engaged experience as not being real even though it is real. Firstly: by defining it as a dream (also meaning not real to you). Secondly: as phantom. You have been doing this as you are now, because of not having to understand how dreams work and that you see the image faintly and not clear—

Okay, meaning?

This means that, every time you sleep and venture to a different dimension, (meaning that when you dream), you think that the event is not real, and also you perceive those who wish and have willed to share the beautiful moment with you as you wish in that dream, as not real, because that is what you think. Also even when they come to you through a leap, in your conscious state that you call reality, you still consider them as phantom, or to simply put it, you say they are ghosts and that they are not real, and not realizing at that moment that they are in a partial state from another dimension or a remote distance of the same realm as thought, that they themselves may not be conscious of in their sleep (when they are dreaming).

Okay, now I think I get it. Just help me out if I am not clear. So from my gathering, you are saying that people in my dreams or things for that matter present themselves or that they are in a partial state from wherever they are. And also, not only are they able to appear in my dream in that state, yet also in this moment I call reality, and they are somewhere sleeping at the same time, and possibly could not be conscious of it, right?

Good, that is exactly what I am saying, child. Yet and also this is for your reality as well, (it is applicable).

Okay, so you saying that ghosts are real?

Well they are not as much as ghosts as you think now, but simply a normal being. They or it—are or it is just as you. You also do the same thing, and if you choose to see and think of them as ghosts, then this makes you one as well, because you go somewhere else in your sleep and appear somewhere, child.

But how am I ghost? I am not dead.

Oh listen, little beauty. The universe is reaching out to you. It is whispering divine truth and you are reading it and hearing in your thoughts from your imagination, now. Choose to be here whole heartedly universal, understand and humble your consciousness for realization. No creation is dead. There is nothing out there even passed beyond your current imagination as it is now, that is dead. In the moment you choose to call life dead, then you are, because you are life itself. Nothing dies. Now therefor listen again. You can as you will, and have as you are now, appear in any state dimension of a dream either partially or totally holistically complete, just like I have said so many times before. You have been and are everywhere you think through thought of imagination in this dream of yours. You are in a dream as we speak through thought, and as you read this right now. You are dreaming, good child. And also this is exactly what I meant, and was explaining on (Death Of Fear). This is all so because you really do not fear death!

Yeah no, I remember Parent, you told me and I understood very clearly.
Good, very good.

Now, since you can and do dream, this means that other people also dream. With this having said, it means that since that you can appear partial, someone else can. Since you are appearing holistically totally physical right now, it means someone is also appearing physically the same right now with you. You can and are, just as you do when you sleep, share the same dream with people (that you favor and choose) in and from other cities, planets, and realm, just as you share your reality now with others (in the very same manner). Yet you do not remember because every time, you visit many different places and have different experiences, of which some of the broader events, people and things that take place, you ignore and are not aware of them, thus when you go back, it feels strange and completely new d é j à vu— to you .

Now getting back to the course of our derailed subject; ghosts as you prefer to call, are real and alive. The being only appears to be in a partial state, thus as such you think it is not real, in your faint imagination—and its own as well. You share and live in the same space with ghosts, or partial beings, yet you do not—

Wait, sorry Parent ⋯ hum, but what about someone I know, I mean someone I have seen die, and then they become ghosts or appear partial in the same place or reality they were ⋯ that means they never went anywhere because their physical bodies will still be in the same realm and also their ghost as well. How does that work?

It just simply means that the body is put to rest and, takes on another form of the physical appearance as either any of its current planetary forms or beings of matter, and that is to say as a rock, tree, animal, water and or etc. as an experience, while its essence dissipate and or travels to another dimension to enter another form as it remembers, thinks and, lurks in the universal dream. Remember child that, when you leave the body, depending whether partially or totally, you tune your frequency to any dimension of state of being, whether in single, dual or multiple dimensional realities.

Oh, yah I remember this as well Parent. It seems like somehow we are going in circles here.

Oh good child, well it is because you have forgotten what you read from what I told, (and you are not adding up the main points). Since you forget, you keep on interrupting and asking same questions of which lies answers for already from past reading. I have explained of what happens when you dream, how and why you dream.

Ah, okay I see. But I can ask if I do have a question right, Parent?

Well yes for sure good child, anytime. Yet see the necessity of it, and remember.

Okay cool, I got it.
Good.

Now, once more again, good child: That which you call a ghost is a partial appearance of a real being from a certain level of tuned frequency from a different other dimension or the same, by their thoughts. What happens is that, the being leaves the body, just like you do every night and day, by putting it to sleep. Yet the body, in this case of a ghost (of what you call a dead person or a being), is left and laid to sleep utterly. After this, only the remains of residual essence live as light frequency of vibration. A being chooses this state when there is no purpose or necessity for it to return or use and experience the physical pleasures of the body that is made of flesh and bones in this reality or planet.

Okay, I understand that Parent. And I actually do because I listened and did not interrupt. Now, I have another question. What about people who get murdered or killed, do they also choose to leave the body by their will?

Everybody does so out of their own will, and you will to do it as well. And you are doing good for asking this, for you are interested in expanding your knowledge. Now listen, for this is where love comes in again just as always. A person who dies, by being murdered by the other, does so out of the will of love. Yes, a person that is killed or murdered leaves the body by their own will choice of experience. Firstly you should grasp the concept of love, for it is broadly ambiguous and oblique.

Mm, okay, I am listening.

Now listen, for this is what love says: There is a soul in the universe in a galaxy on a planet that does not remember being killed, and wishes by desire to know the feeling in experience of how it is. It cries in deep yearning aching calls of thought to the heart to experience what it would love. Through this great universe of dreams, there is yet another part of soul that is listening, hears, and acts out of just love to give what the other wishes, and does not remember killing a being, and it wishes by desire to know the feeling in experience of how it is. It desires so badly to kill, thus it volunteers. Oh, how great and how much it would love to kill—so it offers the experience. Is there anyone or part of a soul being that will give the experience? Now because love is loving, and is unconditional, it understands the true divinity it is. And so it is that love calls forth love in attraction of desire to draw closer. It calls forth both requests experiences of love of being killed and killing, victim and a victimizer. Thus so it is as such that a holy moment of pleasure is experienced by being encountered. It is that as such that a murderer meets the victim. Both parts of souls' desires are fulfilled and completed.

Wow. Once again I do see and understand, Parent. But what kind of soul desires such appalling pleasures of killing? And also what soul wishes to be killed and die anyway?

For the true experience of itself as love, and also it consciously knows that it will not die, and that (NOTHING is going on here), but rather the experience of it, and continue living as a soul being. In your world despite crime being the main reason for murder, there are even those who are rich and wealthy, yet they will to still kill because of love and its adventure of various emotions, that grow from inside. It is because of love that emotions arise; all emotions are created by love. Thus it is as such that when something you love is missing, stolen or has left, you feel anger, hatred, sadness and disappointment towards what has gone or the thing that caused it. So it is as such that one will kill for what they love: either doing it directly personal, or indirectly by sending the other to do it. And also thus it is as such that you feel happy, joyous, glad, fulfilled and great when having gained or given something you love.

Now then, so it is as such that one gets tired of all the continuous struggles and sufferings here, that they ask to be let go of, in pursuit of greater self in another place of dimension; either by pulling the plug off on them, or by throwing themselves into any dying situations, no matter what their condition is.

Ah, oh ⋯ okay, I see. So now tell me, isn't that giving up on life, Parent?

Well it definitely is on this one—in this moment, yet in a broader sense of life it is not, because it is going for a better good option of purpose than the current one, child. You also sometimes leave and let go of things that do not work for you in this life. Letting go is definitely giving up, yet the progress of advancement is measured by whether if you settle for the same or, something you have done before, or something completely new. Now also, you have to remember that it does not die, rather leaves and transcends to another place. And it does this because it has fulfilled its purpose, which in this case is giving their victimizer or a murder the experience of killing, and vice versa—to be killed, or in what they believe in.

Wow, okay ⋯ no, I do see. I understand.
Good, very good my precious kind one.

Wow ⋯ okay, this surely was beyond my understanding. Now tell me one thing here oh good Parent. So you mean even a car accident or any accident of incident also happens willingly. You mean to say that there are no mistakes to death, and that all of this is planned? What I want to know is how and why does it happen that people die, by car accidents, drowning in water, shot by mistake and so on whatever the case of reason may be?

Well, the answer to this is very simple my good friendly child, because it is always love. Once more I will remind you again. It happens because and due to thoughts. It is your thoughts that have created all of this.

Remind me again, please oh good Parent. How?

It is because it happens as it has, that a person thinks casually of distanced events. Taking you for instance in this matter: You have thought by creating in your imagination of being hit or knocked by a car, from simple conversations with someone or just by yourself, by saying something maybe as this, ("just imagine being in a car accident!"). This thought appears not real to you at that moment because you are just casually thinking of it blurry and perceiving it in the future as past experiences, and not experiencing it in the moment, yet you are creating it in existence to a dream as you think it. This is why that by the time the thought is experienced and happens, you normally do not realize it because you are not thinking of it now at that moment, yet you have once thought of it and have created it. And now that it is happening, you would thus say you do not know what happened and that it was not your will or intention because you have forgotten that you thought this through. You forget a lot about what you think, child of love.

Mm ⋯ wow, I do get it. Oh wow, I do ⋯ I do see what you mean, (forgetting to remember knowing). Man! Hum ⋯ I mean woman! Mm ⋯ as hard as it is to believe, I actually believe.

Yes good child. This is exactly why I have cautioned you of your thoughts. Be careful of what you think now in this moment, for you will cause yourself to forget and then blame the experience when it happens to a deity that you do not even know but are creating like we said. And well-done for remembering!

Thanks! Mm ⋯ wow, this does not stop. I mean just when I think you would run out of meaning and reason, yet here you are ⋯ you keep on bouncing back and surprising me by reminding me. But on the real though, I would like to thank you for this realization. I have asked, thus I have received to know. No one has or could explain this in a clear manner like you do now. I now understand. Thank you oh great eternal love.

It is always a pleasure my good lovely and friendly child.

Man, so I have to really monitor and be greatly careful of what I think hey! I mean this is real.

Yes, this is the reality of dreams ⋯ it is real and happening as you think now. Dreams are alive and created by you because you are living—in them—awake.

Man ⋯ I need drink. I just got to digest this all in, you know. Phew, what a read, this is by far most interesting, at least so far I think. Okay, so is this is it, or do you have any more to tell, Parent?

Nah, I am done. You can close the book now. There is nothing to read. Now that you understand, it is over.

Really, Parent?
Got you! I am kidding, you know I would not leave you just like that.

Yeah I know, I have gotten used to your sense of humor. And also I can see that there are few more pages to read, I am not that stupid you know. So yah, what' s next?

Oh there is lot to come, you know this. I mean how many times have I not, child?

Ha hah ⋯ you see! This is exactly the humor I am talking about.

Well of course, I mean it would not be fun if we are serious all the time. Just imagine it child, how it—

Nope ⋯stop right there! I am going to be more careful now, so I won' t imagine that, Parent.

Well done! You do get it now. Even though it is too late for you now, because mentioning it means you have seen it from imagination in your thoughts, yet you are doing good because you are showing progress of being aware and careful. You are evolving the state of yours consciousness. Well done, I am happy for you, child.

Thank you. Okay, now enough with complements and lax talk. Can we get back to business?

Okay sure.

The wind brushes and bypasses with subtle gentle voiced sounds of words. It holds and whispers the truth through to all quarters and corners of the earth and dimensions of the universe in imagery. Oh listen for its truth, see the light through beyond the night for its revelation. Be universally concentric, and be present now my good of a special child for I am resonating eternal truth.

Now listen, for this is what I say. Every day when you wake up, and whatever it is that you do, is been seen, watched, observed and remembered.

I am being watched, by whom?!

Listen, for I am still saying. Therefore more especially of the good and bad things you do, is known. When you do something that someone considers really bad towards them or offensive, that it upsets, and fills them with grudged raged hate of your cause on them, and they do not forget to forgive, you will reap the repercussions of your doings, from the scars of their heart, on how they feel. Because of the very fact that you share, live with and among ghosts (and are one in part as well); the ones that lingers longer that are in relation with and to the person that you have wronged, according to them as they feel, are observing—as you do not see them, in your conscious reality, because of thinking so. So then therefore, for any unpleasant circumstance caused by you to the other, should they strongly acrimoniously feel vengeance, and punishment to be reciprocated from their heart, it will and can be carried by their dead loved ones that are now spiritual ghosts, on the same planet, space and dimension you are in, if and when they feel to do so.

Wait, so now even ghosts are out to get me, Parent?

Well yes, yet only for revenge of what you or your family lineage has done, either for themselves or for their loved ones, when they feel to do so. And these are what you call gods-ancestors, because they protect and shield you, from unconscious reality and events.

Mm, I see, very interesting. But why do I have to or should I be punished for something that my great grandparent did, Parent?

Your parents and the great alike, start fights, wars and quarrels with their neighbors, colleagues, friends, strangers and even family and etc. from jealousy and misunderstanding. Now because your great have killed, injured, wounded and stolen from someone's child, and have caused sheer pain and grief on them, yet they themselves have not felt, they will thus feel it through their great children. It is because the one that passes on (dies), promise themselves and do not forget what your great parents did. They make this promise when still alive, and when it cannot be met or done in that period of moment when they are alive (as physical bodies), they seek to make you or your family experience what they did, from your family. Yet this does not happen often, and is not always the case with all spiritual ghosts of beings, because some make peace, and are drawn to other better different experiences of other dimensions that can be turned worse. Is it not that you have felt and sought to avenge someone to get back at them in some form or another, at some time? So as such that as long as you have that grudge, you will carry it on until you let go, no matter how or on what cost you accept or feel. And so it is that a ghost still holds a grudge!

Mm ⋯ Okay, I get that as well, wow.

Now, because ghosts are in a light partial state, they can travel fast to anywhere in all the dimensions or place they think, at any moment, by instant transmission. Therefore wherever you are, you shall be found, and vengeance

195

will be carried out as felt, desired and or subliminally unconsciously requested by the victim of your action. This is the reason why you find very most often that, something that you did on to the other comes back to you in an unusual and rather in a very unexpected manner, yet familiar. It is so because of ghosts, and the message sont from the heart through thought by the victim in prayer in moment. Even when the person you have wronged has passed on, when they feel to cause you grief that you have given them through their physical moments by haunting you, they will do so, until they are satisfied, and or you have done right by them, and or to their (remaining) living loved ones.

Yet and also, you are protected as well. You are defended by your own ancestors. This then becomes a war between what you have named gods and ancestors, to and for you. It literally becomes a spiritual war. Yet when you have done bad and wrong, and have caused unbearable grievous moments to any of those who have passed—, (from your family' s side), and they have hated you for it, they will mostly choose not to help or protect you when you are in danger, either with other ghosts or normal people or events.

Now listen, for this will help you. Yet when you do good to a person, whenever their spiritual ghost encounters you in danger, wherever you may be, it will remember the good you did, and will serve protectively in favor for that one great thing you did to them. And when you are good to everybody, no harm, yet goodness and mercy shall follow according to your deeds.

Mm, I hear you my good Parent. Now tell me here, then why is that some people who seem to have lived a good decent life, experience bad things they do not deserve, and even die tragic deaths?

Mm … I see you have forgotten. It is because they choose their experience, yet I do understand your question, my great child, and I will answer it accordingly.

196

Firstly, you do not know (have forgotten) what that person does or did. How they present themselves to you is and can be different from how they present themselves away from you or how they were. Now, this simply means that you do not know the past experiences of that person's life, from another realm or dimension. A person does something in an else other realm, and comes to this one, trying to forget their past. And like I have said that a spiritual ghost can travel anywhere to any place as it wills instantly as long as it knows where it is going. Therefore this is thus as such that your great past still comes for you, this is why apparently a decent seeming person would be in a tragedy. This is all because it is a dream (and you have nowhere to run, because there is only one dream), you can and will do whatever you want in a dream. There are no rules but yours. We are in a dream and all is possible. Remember that all is real!

Mm, and that is true Parent. Yes, I do remember that.
Good. Now we move on.

Live a dream

Oh my great dreamer: The one that has forgotten true pleasure of self and creation. A dream is all that you have in this life of the universe, and it is sparkling and floating around in awesomeness, and revealing its beauty fantastically. It is the sweet taste of honey that flows through as the fresh springs that fall down on a mountain like twinkling stars quenching the thirst of the universe. It is the one that pumps your heart desire in passionate power for achieving self-greatness within, to glorify its true nature.

A dream is a blue print of your identity and origin. It is the only thing that is keeping you alive and striving for who and what you are. Therefore be nothing else but your dream. A dream is impregnated with you, and it produces fragments of true deepest desires that are pleasurable, of and about

197

yourself. Dance and shout, scream out your feelings in the open, spin around and jump frolicking throwing your hands in the skies to scatter crumpled fragmented dust of gold and diamonds of your dream and, let them pour and sprinkle on your skin and decorate your beauty with gleams of sun as it falls on fertile grounds to flourish and recreate itself. This is your dream, and a dream is love making. Make love to your dream, now, by loving it and yourself. This is dreams of love.

Now listen, child. This is the right time to be in the moment, be still and conscious in this reality of your dream. This is the moment of being aware of who you are and, what you choose to create. Now this is what I say: You desire to have all knowledge and understanding of everything, be it and, have it. You desire to have great fame and fortune along with wealth, so have and be it. You desire to be noble and help others, so have and be it. You desire to have peace and lead a slow quite life with family, so have and be it. You desire to be good at what you do and love, so have and be it. Be only this, that which you desire deeply and nothing else other. A great dreamer, and that is to say the one that creates and makes a dream greater, just as you are, is the one that understands and realizes that he or she or it is a creator.

For you to be able to experience and express a great part of your now dream, you would have to choose to let go of all the other parts, which you think are not great in this moment of your now living dream. By doing this, you acquire only a lot of that one part of your dream, thus it becomes great, and you become as it is.

Now listen, child, this is how you live a dream. Every day and time, when you wake up and open your eyes—only see, be and do your dream. Your first thoughts, leading to words in your awoken state of and to the day, should speak your dream. The very first step of walk should be in line with your dream. Everything and anything has, should and must be about your dream willingly out of unconditional love. And also, again, every day and time, when you sleep and close your eyes—only see, be and do your dream. Your first thoughts, leading to creative imagination in your awoken state of sleep of the day and night, should speak your dream. Do this all the time and you will see what great results are produced.

Wow, now that is quite inspiring, but will I not be tired from doing the same thing, over and over as many times over again, Parent?

Surely one does get fatigued, and the body feels to rest from all the strains that you pull it through. Yet you never get tired from doing what you love in this moment, no matter how long the span of the moment is (because what you love is so big), you do not ever get tired, child!

Okay ⋯ whoa, now, wait. I never get tired, especially from doing what I love? Yes, you do not.

Okay⋯ I am just waiting on you to explain ⋯

Good, now this is what I am saying. Being tired can and, may be understood in two ways if not less or more, by choice. Firstly: yes, too much of a good thing is the same as bad, and this is to say that, doing more of the same thing over and over again is tiring. Yet when you rest from a thing that you have done over and over again, and in your sleep or rest, you then suddenly imagine a great helpful idea that will help towards what you have rested from, and then wake up again, to do what you have dreamt or thought, and add it towards what you had rested from—that does not make or mean that you are or were tired from it, because you still do it in other parts of this one dream.

You are not tired from it, because you are still in the process of completing it —in the process of creation by having ideas about it in your dream and awaken realized state. Therefore you never get tired in a dream. Now if you were really tired as you claim, then you would not even have any slight idea

199

that contributes towards that thing you have rested from, which is your life—right now, and what you are doing.

Now listen again. Also when you rest or sleep from a thing that you have done over and over again, and you do not create, imagine or think and have any ideas that contributes to what you were doing, then it means that you hate and you do not love what you are doing, and it is exhausting you. It exhausts you so badly that it drains your energy and causes you to be uncreative, thus waking up again to try and figure out what it is that you love in your dream and, end up doing the same thing again because you had no idea in your creative imagination because you did not find it in your sleep.

Wow ⋯ phew! You know what? You sometimes make feel stupid. I mean, I feel like I ask questions that are so obvious, especially to you, yet I do not know how to form the answers. And I am afraid that somehow I feel like people are watching and that I am on world's stage. And here I am revealing how stupid and lame I am, Parent!

Well I tell you this, child. Every time you say and do something and—walk by that road, just know that someone is looking and watching you. And that someone is of and from this world just as you are, thus as such people of this world will always wonder what you are up to ⋯ and are you living your dream and becoming the person you said and promised yourself are in your dream as you said you would—in this moment? Therefore this is a stage ⋯ you are on world stage, and are you performing or not, child?

Okay ⋯ I see. I really do see. Thank you for opening my eyes, Parent.
You are welcomed child, you are all welcomed!

Now listen to this, child. For a dream to be fully experienced, there is no wanting. This means that to ultimately make a dream a reality, there is only creation. This is to say that you only create, and what you create produces what you have already, from inside of you, (rather than wanting to have it outside of you), because wanting gives a defined meaning to reality that you do not have. Want is particular and it does definitely create reality of experiencing lack—therefor it is real.

You see child, want is experienced blur, tinted and faded reality of your true ultimate dream. The experience is blur because you do not see yourself in your dreams clearly as you clearly see yourself, and what you have now, from having produced it by creating it. Want is unclear because you are still trying to figure out if, you really are going to produce that which you desire, yet you are not sure because you are unclear if you will produce, do it or have what you desire because you do not see the image properly due to blurriness. Therefore thus as such that you say that you only want a thing, and it does not matter if you have it or not because you have created a knowing fact that you might or might not do or have it, because you are sure that you can' t see it clearly.

Now, the only way to produce what you want, is to be aware and realize that you want it. After realizing that you want it, from your desires, you thus stop immediately, wanting it, instead produce it by, creating it using miscellaneous imagination to have it called your own, in your reality. Now this is what I say, once having wanting something, stop wanting it more because you will keep on wanting, instead create it more and you will have more of it, in creation.

Oh okay ⋯ wow, so I should not want anything, Parent?

Now listen, child. Yes you should want anything or something, because want makes you realize your desires, yet having realized what your desire is, from wanting it, do not want it anymore instead create it, then thus will you produce having it!

Wow, I do hear you, Parent. I really do hear you, that is great news. And I will always say and let you know that I am thankful and grateful for such great wisdom you have given unto me. Thank you.

It is always a pleasure, and you are always welcomed, child. And always know that you are doing good!

Now I say and tell you this: That moment that you always have ⋯ that intrinsic pertinent driving power of passion to what you desire that expresses your nature; that is your dream talking to you. That is you wholly fully talking to yourself from inside. It is your hunger from and of yourself. You want, wish, desire to burst out of yourself (your own skin) as who you truly are in this moment. Therefore stop holding yourself from yourself and reveal yourself. Do you know how powerful you are? Do you know what marvelous great creation you can produce! You are the one, in this dream, that has everything. Look child—you see that? That is all yours. Look! Over yonder, that is yours too!

Everything, by creating it, is yours! Now, no matter what, listen to that inner voice more than your external voice. I tell you this, you will, cannot and may never let yourself down doing yourself and, what you love because you are not expecting anything and you are not cynical or judging yourself.

I hear you parent. But why is it, and has it taken such a good while to have that car of my dream, that house and my best companion along with family of my dream? Why is the process so slow?

Now listen, child. Like I have said before, everything that you have now with you, is because you said thank you to it by accepting it and saying that it is a pleasure. Now, the things that you desire, such as your house, car and your best companion and children, do take and, have taken a good while because you were not clear about yourself. You want many things of which you are not sure you can have (by your own imagination). Yet once you have and, totally know and are sure as clear of who you are, just as you are right now, things start to and have fallen to right positions in your now dream, child.

Now listen to this, as well, my good child. Once immediately you know yourself, who and what you choose and want to be in your life of your dream, you will not want that which is not. Therefore only choosing your dream produces exactly that—(your dream). Wanting any or many other things, destruct and distract from the original clarity of who you are, and what you want. These many things that are added later, confuses and draws your attention towards them, thus you focus on rectifying, rather than living as you are, already in your dream—which is being great and awesome.

Mm ⋯ that is true Parent. Now tell me, why was I not clear about myself, and who I want to be in my dream since from birth or young?

The truth is, child, you were always clear about who you are and what your dream is, now, in this current life of yours, and just had forgotten as you are remembering now, to know now.

Oh yah, yes ⋯ I do remember that, forgetting to remember knowing. Well this is to remind myself that I know everything I choose and to experience.

Yes, that is exactly it my good one.

Now, again, just like I have said before. You distract yourself with many other things that you desire. You always know and knew what your passion is, and what you are really good at and love, at the same time. You know and knew this, and you never expected anything from anybody by doing it, because you did it out of love, and it was, just as it is now, who you simply are. When you are young, you change your mind a lot. You realize that there are many things that can be done, the word impossible merely exists in your vocabulary and consciousness—(and not only can they be done), but also be achieved, by will —your will. In doing this, you never decide on one thing, but rather tried things out to see if they are to your liking (because they were possible to do), away from your first clear and, loved packaged part of your desire in this whole entire created dream of yours because it was as it is possible to do all of them.

Mm ⋯ home run, this is also true, Parent! I mean I did try out a few things, mainly because I thought I could be, and that they can be achieved. Yet of all those things; I am experiencing just only this, which is what I have now.

And you can still achieve the ones you desire to experience, my beloved one.

I can?
Yes you can and will, child. That is guaranteed by the universe!

Now, remember this. A dream is yours and, it is for you. Whatever you do, in this moment, is your dream. Therefore, now, you should choose not to be hasty in and, for your dream. Everything that you do, should be done in caution and clear consciousness. You have all the time to develop and work towards your dream, child.

I hear you, Parent. But now, is it not going to slow me down in life, again, just as it took me a good awhile to understand, and figure out all of this, of who I am, and what dreams are? I mean my peers and other people will be ahead of me, they will have advanced way ahead of me.

Good, well enough. Now I tell you this: a dream is not competitive. It is not competitive because there is only it, just one dream, and all of you are in it. All life and creation is a dream, therefore it is not competing against itself. For you to have worry at this moment, now, it shows that you are still not clear of who you are, hence you are worried of your peers being ahead of you.

Remember that once you are sure and clear of who you are, you will not even have the slightest of doubt and worry.

Now listen to this again, child. All money, all wealth and pleasures of desires and friendship will come and go, and yet one thing will remain, and that is your dream—your creative process of things. I tell you this, a dream produces all the desires. You do not have to worry about anything else because your dream will produce it, and yet anything else will not produce a dream because it is all that is, already. When there is no money, wealth, health and pleasure, you are only left with your dream. You are only left with the one thing through which you are able to imagine and create, and put to being your thoughts.

Being creative and imaginative does not require riches and wealth, but only your dream. Your dream creates from your imagination, and thus draws the riches and wealth that you have bargained with what you have created and imagined from your dream. Whatever it is that you produce from your dream, can as it will, be exchanged or traded for wealth and or riches. This can be done as it is, by putting a value of worth on to your creation to gain wealth. Therefore this simply means that there is first creation of something from your dream in your imagination, and it attracts wealth according to the standard value of worth you have put on to it.

Wow, okay I see Parent.

Now listen, for this is how you live a dream. For everything that you wish and desire in your now dream, only say what is. I repeat again: only say what is. By this I mean, only say the things that are, and not the ones that are not.

I' m sorry what, Parent?

Listen to what I am saying, for I am again yet giving you another obvious secret that you have chosen to neglect from your ignorance. I am giving here, right now, the most powerful words to create what is.

Okay ⋯ I' m good and set to go, please tell me.

Now, the first word of three that add up to six letters is, *I*.
I ⋯ Parent?

Yes, *I*. *I* is the most powerful assigning word of creation that declares and identifies you as you are. Everything that you want, especially that of your dream, should be declared as you will, by using *I*. When you use *I*, it means that you account and become fully responsible for what follows after *I*—as in you. Without *I*, no ownership and claim of any desire will be had by you. *I*, refers and points directly to the one source that creates by thought, word and deed—to be.

Now I tell you this, whatever it is that you wish for, you should choose to put yourself before that desire by declaring that you are it, by putting the word *I*. This means that when you say or use the word or letter *I*, you are saying what is, and this refers to you being that which is. Therefore my good child, to live and have your dream lived totally and have your desires, in this now moment, always call things to you that are, by saying "I ...", because *I* is who you are, and thus makes you what is as you are.

Okay I hear you Parent. So whenever I want something, I must just use the word or letter or the alphabet *I*?

Not only in wanting, and also in declaring. You see child, *I* declares your state of being and who you are in the moment as you see yourself in your dream. *I* is your identity.

206

Okay ··· I see and understand.

Good, very good, child. I also see and notice that you understand, because you have used *I* in your words of sentence, you have just said, "Okay ··· I see and understand". Therefore sight and understanding has been assigned to you, for you have used *I*.

Okay ··· so it's like that, just like that? That seems so easy to do, I can deal with that.

Well I am glad you find it easy, yet the truth is that you have been struggling to use the word *I* appropriately, to attract and draw the things that are part of your dream. And you will find it a bit difficult to use and say it in days to come before you master it.

What do you mean by that, Parent?

Well you have used *I* to summon and attract things that distract you in your dream. You have called things upon you and even declared them by saying and using the word *I*. You have said and declared things such as, "I am broke," "I do not have money at all," "I have nothing," "I am so drunk," "I have stolen this," "I have slept with that person," "I have a second hand item," "I do not know," "I do not see how this is going to work." You even say that you are a cleaner, a waiter, or a person working in an office for someone. All of these have been declared to soon later realize that what you have pointed to you, some of it is no more of liking just as useless as its absence. This means that you wanted things by using *I*, and soon later to regret having them. You regret because you see that having them does not help in achieving that which you desire the most in relation to your dream.

Okay, I got that. So what is the next word after, *I*. You said that there are three, right?

Yes, indeed there are, child. Yes there are.

The second word correlatively is **AM**. **AM** after *I*, creates a significant produce in your dream, and is very important. Just like *I—*, **AM**, also assigns things directly to you, and it mostly correlates with *I*. Therefore *I* and **AM**, are used dependently concomitant to each other to produce and manifest a certain particular reality about yourself as declared. You see, my good child, whenever you say "*I AM*" , you instantly become that which you say you are in this moment by thought and word as you have spoken it.

Wait, so whenever I say '*I AM*' , I instantly become, Parent?

Yes you do child, by thought and word, only in that moment of saying and doing, until you say you are something else (of which you are now not or were)—in the very same moment and time. That is why you should choose to all the time, say only who you are and what is in your dream, in the moment. And the longer you keep that moment, the longer you stay that which you say you are and do, by actually being. Only say the things that make and complete you in your dream, child. You want, wish and dream being something particular ⋯ all you have to say is *I AM* ⋯, whatever it is that you will say you are, and you become one, in that moment. Therefore choose to not ever use the word **NOT** upon who you are and the things you want and wish to be. Choose not to use **NOT**! For it is who you are not.

Wait? What! I should choose not to use the word **NOT**? I do not understand, I mean how does this relate to defining who or what I am and what we are talking about?

Oh my good dreamer, my one and only child that lives life to the fullest of its dream. When you say, "I am *NOT*," you create an aspect reality of dream that you are what you say you are not. It means you think yourself being it that which you say you are not in this moment (as you imagine what you are not), and thus resist the very idea as you have thought it, of being it by saying you are not it. This simply means that, you imagine and bring to life by creating an idea that defines you in your dream, and repudiate by resisting it because of not liking the created idea by saying you are not. So then, when you say or use the word, *NOT*, it means you deny what you have created of yourself idealistically from previous choice of thought in your imagination and experience. Therefore you resist who you are.

Remember that whenever you say and use the word *I* and *AM*, you assign things to you in your dream, thus you become what you are not, now, in a certain point of space in the universe by creating the very realistic idea of it as you think imaginatively, in that moment (of who you are not!). Remember that this is a dream, and everything is possible and you are awake in it as you witness what is before you as it unfolds. Remember that you are everywhere and only experiencing what you have crystalized, of all parts of your being in space. And what you see as you envisage, is real as seen by being physically crystalized; by saying what you see in your vision.

Yah, I do remember Parent.
Good, very good.

Yes my good child. Only say who and what you are and what is, in your dream.

This is all bewildering, Parent. I mean it seems to be such great effort to say and do this all the time. And how do you say and do this anyway, by not involving, *NOT*, all the time, and saying what is?

Say only what you are and what is, in every moment of this moment.

But how, it seems impossible to not use the word **NOT**. I mean if I am not, I am not, right?

Yes indeed you are what you say you are not, of which you were once, child. You see, exactly my point, this is perplexing, Parent.

Okay my lovely one, this is how you do it and say it. When you choose not to be or go somewhere, choose not to say that you are not going there, instead rather say where you are going or where you are remaining or staying. This means that you should choose to say by your will that— "I am staying behind," or "I am going to ⋯" whatever and wherever the place may be that you are going to. Only name and say what you will be doing, and mention not what you chose not to do or be in this moment as it progresses to define.

For instance: you have said, "I don't mean to ⋯" , "It is not that I don't ⋯" , "it is not because ⋯" , "I am not trying to ⋯" and followed by such words as, be rude, steal, run away, hide from you, I hate you, sleep with you, have sex, I am jealous, kind, I am polite and or I love you. You say that you are not saying, doing or being, yet in the same moment (you are saying, doing and being what you say you are not). You say you do not mean to be rude to someone by actually saying rude things to them—as you have said out loud already and or even thought. You suggest sexual signals to someone by words, and actions and, say that you are not trying to have sex or sleep with them. You say that you are not trying to be kind or polite to someone, yet doing a kind and or a polite thing them. Therefore in this sense, you are what you say you are not. When something is not, it is not and therefore does not have to be mentioned or done as it is not.

Mm ⋯ yes ⋯ wow, I do see and understand, Parent. But you are using the word **NOT**, most of the time if not all the time. You have mentioned and told

210

me of the things I should choose not to do, by actually you saying and using the word **NOT**, just as now. So is this even possible, how am I supposed to do all of this when you are not?

Yes my good child, you are correct and right and, I will tell you why. I tell you this, it is because of the limitation of words that I have and had to use **NOT**, to make you understand. When and if I would have said what is, all the time, earlier on when you started reading this, you would have been perplexed, baffled and not clear, and asking many more questions just as you have and are now. All of this of what you are reading now, would have begun and ended on a single paragraph. Even a paragraph seems to be of a great length; it would have actually began and ended with just three words.
Wait, what—you mean all of this reading and information would be summarized in three words?

Yes good child, and I am explaining them now.

Okay ⋯ and what do you mean that I would have not understood, Parent, and how do you even know? Why don' t you give me a try first? Are you undermining me?

Okay, anything to please you, child. Yet now you will understand, because I have explained things to you thoroughly (already), with the use of what is not.

Okay I hear you, Parent.

Now here is what is: there is only you in the universe. The next person you meet is you, and everything of anything is you. It is forever that I am you, and you are I AM. For you are I AM, you are thus the great that I AM—and indeed you are the great I AM. You are entitled to as many as I AM.

I am the wind. I am the fertile soil that forms rocks and objects of particles that creates them. I am the creature and specie of all kinds of beings. I am the nourishing water that multiplies. I am the light created in the dark and the space it travels through, that houses the universes. I am in the past, future and present. I am love that created to hate itself in exhaustion to destruction, jealousy, anger, pride, arrogance, violence, understanding, happiness, joy, kind, humble, and exhibition of great unmatched glorious power to myself in expression, to death to live in inexistence of fear of what I am. I AM THE GREAT I AM.

Come on, Parent. I do understand exactly what you are saying. I mean I sort of get you, in a way. So is that all there is, I mean is that all that is?

Yes, and like I have said, it is actually three words of what is, child.
Oh yah, I remember you said that. So what is not?

From what you have just read, whatever is not there is not, child?

Hum ··· ah ··· okay let me check to see. Hum ··· there seems to be everything, I mean I personally for one can't find anything that is not.

Well that is good, child.

Wait if that's all there is and what is, where does all of the stuff that is not come from and how does it be?

It is because what is, says that it is not! It changes what it is by denying itself for anew.

Alright, I have that. Now what is the next word?

NOW!

212

NOW, Parent?

Yes, *NOW*! *I* and *AM*, used together gives the definition. Yet the experience is had through *NOW*. You may say that you are whatever you say you are, yet you will only experience that, the moment you decide to become it, and that is *NOW*. Therefor this means you can be and are anything. What is important is when you will experience that which you already are. Whatever it is in life, and whenever you want it, you should always use and call it now. No matter how far and where it is, only because you have called it, now, it will as it is already, be on the way. Therefore, *NOW*, is what you are doing. And whatever it is that you are doing now, you are it. At this moment you are a reader of these great notes (you are now reading this!).

This is to confirm that, when you work on yourself, especially your dream, your future starts to take place now the moment you do it. Hence the saying, "the future is *NOW*." Yet you, my special child, have shifted *NOW*. Your life has become a bit slow especially on the creative productive side, because of how you use *NOW*, in your world, of this dream. In most moments, you have and still do get great solutions and ideas to your life that are so brilliant, yet you shift them and put them on hold. This you do it through the power of time that you have fallen for and accepted.

This is to say that you may think to do something, yet you hold it back by saying that you will do it tomorrow. And when tomorrow seems to not be enough, because you are abstracted and distracted by small minor activities; you then set goals for yourself in the far distanced future that you call dream or goal that need to be achieved, by not even realizing that you are already living it now. You say that you would like to be someone of some type in five or ten years. By this factual reality that you set before yourself, you then wait or slowly progress before you become whatever it is that you are thinking of, *NOW*. And while still in progression, you then sometimes change your mind, (of which when that five or ten years arrive—, you are not!) and if that is not all, something happens to you by your own chance of letting. This is to say that you let fate take its toll on you, and willingly take whatever is thrown at you, by choice. It is because of stopping and breaking **NOW**, and withholding from it, that you forget to do something. A thing comes to mind that you should do, yet you hold it back, and say to yourself that you will do it later, and by the time later comes, you have forgotten and are doing something else other.

NOW is a very powerful term and moment. Whatever it is that you have forgotten, or done in the past, the moment you remember it, it will be and is **NOW**. Therefore when it comes to mind the moment of thinking about it, it should be done, because now you are thinking about it, even if it was in the past and you had forgotten of it. Yet this has become a difficult exercise for you because you are many things idealistically (from your thoughts), and have not ultimately decided on one that you really are. Now I tell you this: it is all changing, because I am giving you the greatest manipulative answer as solution. Choose your love, and this is to say what you love. Value it to a great grand degree. See this image all the time now, and you shall be. Say thank you for it, for your prayer has been heard. Know this and choose not to forget it. Fear not, for it is dead (fear is dead) because you passed past it. Oh my great love, the one I cherish to my soul, claim yourself with this great gift I have given to you.

Choose to use the answers that you have asked for, for greater purpose of self until you become selfless. Now, this is how you do it. Every time observe the moment and place you are at, and ask yourself why am I here, and what am I doing now? When you do this, you will always have the answer as to who you are. You will be able to answer yourself without my help for you will now know and understand, by seeing that whether you are or not, that which you say you are. And whenever not, you will definitely know what to do for all is written.

Oh my flower, because of that everything that you do, in every moment, you choose, want, and are doing it better, and greater than before, you are thus great every time. This is thus as such that you are the great *I AM* that is *NOW*. You are the great that you are now. And this is all that you have to say to yourself: *"I AM THE GREAT I AM—NOW!"* When you realize this, you are releasing pure true power of being who you are greatly, in the moment. This is how a dream is lived and experienced. This is how you live a dream. All you have to say is *I AM NOW*, and live what you say you are the moment you say it, now!

I AM NOW

www.ingramcontent.com/pod-product-compliance
Lightning Source LLC
LaVergne TN
LVHW011224080426
835509LV00005B/306